ENDORSE

I hold Canon Andrew White in the highest regard. He walks in a level of faith, humility, honor, and courage few achieve in this world. He demonstrates that when we live like Jesus did on the earth, fully dependent on the Father, we have access to power from on high.

The stories of his Iraqi believers, those who gave their lives as martyrs, especially the passionate, faith-filled children, remind me of my courageous Mozambican family. I also know brave believers who have literally laid their lives down for the Gospel or forgiven those who murdered their families. One graduation day, we were commissioning our new pastors and sending them back to their villages during a time of heavy conflict. We all knew some might be returning to be martyrs, and we could feel the holy, sovereign weight on that moment. Others from our team also went to the conflict areas to share the Gospel and support the believers.

As Andrew testifies throughout this phenomenal book, it is true that when Jesus is all you have, He truly becomes all you need. As you read these pages, remember that the Triune God who performed each and every miracle in the Middle East is the very same God you serve. You also have access to the river of His Presence and the power of Holy Spirit. Let these powerful testimonies build your faith, encourage your heart, and inspire you to give everything for this glorious Gospel.

HEIDI G. BAKER, PH.D
Co-founder and Executive Chairman of Iris Global

I can only hope that Canon Andrew White's book *Glory Zone in the War Zone* will inspire in you, dear reader, as passionate and desperate a quest for more of the manifest Glory of God as it has done in me. This truly is an amazing book. The "Vicar of Baghdad" has a "Glory story" to tell!

JOHN ARNOTT
Catch the Fire Ministries, Toronto

Our God is the God of the impossible. And, because of the nature of the Father, it is in our DNA to invade every hopeless situation. Reverend Andrew White's new book, *The Glory Zone in the War Zone,* powerfully depicts this reality. These pages reveal a man who carries unique boldness and faith as he shepherds God's people, bringing His kingdom in the midst of war-torn Iraq. His testimonies are not meant to remain in Baghdad, though. Each story of divine provision, protection, and restoration is a witness of God's nature. They declare the glory available to every believer in any situation. Read this book as a description of your inheritance in the kingdom. In it, you will find a beautifully challenging depiction of how God sees this troubled nation and His definition of the normal Christian life.

BILL JOHNSON
Bethel Church, Redding, CA
Author of *The Way of Life* and *Hosting the Presence*

This extraordinary new book from Canon White is a tremendous gift to all those seeking powerful insights into spiritual leadership. These lessons, literally forged in spiritual gold out of the dust of despair and brokenness experienced in the Middle East, will send you back to your first love with renewed passion; back to the vital principles of genuine prayer, praise, and uninhibited faith in God when there is no other help but in the name of Yeshua of Nazareth.

I urge you to become friends with "Abouna" (Father) Andrew and benefit from his rewarding, often heart-breaking instruction toward a more mature, effective walk in the living reality of Messiah.

BEN VOLMAN
Messianic Rabbi, Kehillat Eytz Chaim, Toronto
Vice-President of the Union of Messianic Jewish Congregations

Canon Andrew White is a man after God's own heart. He lives to love God with all his heart, mind, and strength, to love his neighbor as he loves himself, and to love and pray for his enemies. In this book we see how this kind of love drives out all fear and gives extraordinary courage to enter war zones and release God's glory while enabling people to become instruments of peace and forgiveness instead of weapons of war. I met Andrew in 2004 when reporting on the Iraq war for Fox News. He was hard at work ministering in Baghdad and the Middle East working relentlessly in pursuit of peace. In the midst of heartbreak and terror, Canon White holds up the banner of God's love and releases the presence of Jesus.

KELLY WRIGHT
Former Fox news reporter/news anchor
for Baghdad, Basrah, and Mosul

Andrew's thrilling account of the vibrant reality of life in the Glory Zone is a passionate testimony of God's love and deliverance for His people in the most desperate of circumstances.

Having served with US Forces in Baghdad, I understand much of what Andrew and the wonderful congregation of St. George's endured. It was, for them, infinitely more dangerous than for us in the military, and their faith in adversity is astounding and humbling.

I had the privilege of worshiping with Andrew throughout my year's tour of duty, sitting under his ministry. We experienced exactly what he argues—that where there is worship, God's throne is established. Our God is a shield and protector for His people, a worker of miracles in difficult times. This book describes that where there is pain and desperation, there is also grace and blessing in great measure. God's power and His sovereign ability to deliver is writ large throughout this book, and this book resounds to our heavenly Father's glory.

MAJOR GENERAL RODDY PORTER, MBE
CEO, Military Ministries International

In this amazing new book, Andrew White tells us how he experienced the Glory of God through remarkable phenomena accompanying his work in the Middle East. Many times, when things appeared impossible, God showed up. At the end of each chapter, Andrew has written a personal prayer for us, the readers. Just as Andrew regularly takes inspiration from Smith Wigglesworth's simplicity of life with its profound ministry, here we can learn about Andrew's life and testimony of how God confirmed His Glory in the Middle East with accompanying miracles, signs, and wonders.

Andrew's selflessness and life committed to being available to help the suffering people in the Middle East will not go *down* in history; it will go *up* to the Glory of his Savior!

I have found this book extremely encouraging and strengthening.

DR. HENRY FARDELL
Dental surgeon and great-grandson of Smith Wigglesworth

GLORY ZONE

— IN THE —

WAR ZONE

MIRACLES, SIGNS, AND WONDERS
IN THE MIDDLE EAST

ANDREW WHITE

DESTINY IMAGE® PUBLISHERS, INC.

P.O. Box 310, Shippensburg, PA 17257-0310

"Promoting Inspired Lives."

This book and all other Destiny Image and Destiny Image Fiction books are available at Christian bookstores and distributors worldwide.

Cover design by Eileen Rockwell
Interior design by Terry Clifton

For more information on foreign distributors, call 717-532-3040.

Reach us on the Internet: www.destinyimage.com.

ISBN 13 TP: 978-0-7684-5318-8
ISBN 13 eBook: 978-0-7684-5319-5
ISBN 13 HC: 978-0-7684-5321-8
ISBN 13 LP: 978-0-7684-5320-1

For Worldwide Distribution.
1 2 3 4 5 6 7 8 / 24 23 22 21 20

I dedicate this book to my beloved mother, Pauline White—*A woman of worship and unwavering faith, a woman of the glory.*

Acknowledgements

I thank my heavenly Father for His unfailing love, faithfulness, and kindness and for His precious Son and Holy Spirit—my greatest teachers.

I thank my beloved wife, Caroline, and my sons, Josiah and Jacob, and my dear mother and sister, Pauline and Joanna—all such treasured gifts of God who have always been a strength and inspiration to me.

I am also deeply grateful to all of the key individuals in churches and in media who have supported me in fulfilling the call of God on my life, especially David Armstrong who mentored me in my early years of training for ministry.

I thank my Iraqi people who have always fixed their eyes on Jesus and shared in the living reality of the glory zone in the war zone. I am ever grateful to each one of them, young and old, for showing me what real faith and unity look like. We have walked together on mountaintops and through valleys.

I thank the many churches, leaders, friends, and supporters from all over the world who have enabled me to provide both spiritually and practically for my people and who have stood with the persecuted church in relentless prayer, compassion, and sincerity.

I also express my sincere gratitude to my team in the UK and the Middle East who continue to strengthen and encourage me in all of my work, particularly in supporting my Iraqi Christian Community now residing in Jordan. Amongst them, my deepest thanks must go to my Middle East director, Fr. Carlos Khalil Jaar, and my chairman of trustees, Mr. Martyn Keates and those who have travelled with me and supported me nationally and internationally in this recent season, Rachael, Jake, Esther, Jesse, Callum, and Dan.

I am deeply grateful to Larry Sparks for taking time out of his busy schedule to meet me in London, to Bill Williams for his friendship and encouragement, to Owen Rowlands for his artistic insights, and, last but not least, to all of the Destiny Image team who have worked faithfully and skillfully in enabling this work to be published for such a time as this.

To God be all the glory!

—The Reverend Canon, DR. ANDREW WHITE

CONTENTS

FOREWORD   *by Mahesh Chavda*........................ 1

CHAPTER ONE   The Glory Zone 3

CHAPTER TWO   Prophetic Influences 13

CHAPTER THREE   The Glory in the Bethlehem Siege 25

CHAPTER FOUR   Radical Divine Reversal 39

CHAPTER FIVE   Sovereign Provider...................... 55

CHAPTER SIX   Experiencing Tangible Glory 69

CHAPTER SEVEN   The Man in White....................... 77

CHAPTER EIGHT   Angels in Our Midst.................... 87

CHAPTER NINE   The God Who Goes Before Us........... 95

CHAPTER TEN   Kingdom's Children, Children's Kingdom . 109

CHAPTER ELEVEN   Resurrection Glory 123

CHAPTER TWELVE   The Great Name....................... 131

CHAPTER THIRTEEN   People of Covenant 141

CHAPTER FOURTEEN   Martyrdom and Allegiance............. 151

CHAPTER FIFTEEN   Glory in the Word..................... 171

CHAPTER SIXTEEN   Worship: He is Worthy of It All 181

CHAPTER SEVENTEEN   The Glory of the Shepherd.............. 191

CONCLUSION   The River in the War Zone 209

FOREWORD

IT HAS BEEN MY GREAT PRIVILEGE TO BE ABLE TO CALL THE "Vicar of Baghdad," Canon Andrew White, a close, dear friend. Over the years, I would often find him in the middle of some major world crisis where I would witness the supernatural grace God has given to this servant and ambassador of peace. I recall getting a phone call late one night in 2002. It was Andrew calling from the West Bank where he was the chief negotiator for the Archbishop of Canterbury during the siege of the Church of the Nativity. I answered my phone to hear Andrew's voice, "Mahesh, we are at an impasse. Do you have a word from the Lord?"

Despite struggling with MS for years, Canon Andrew White has been at the center of great events in the Middle East, carrying an apostolic voice of counsel and shalom into some of the darkest situations. Whether negotiating an international crisis or setting up humanitarian aid in a besieged city, Andrew is tuned into the voice of the Lord and a carrier of miracle glory in impossible situations.

1

I have seen few who walk with such a zeal for God and His people under such dangerous conditions. During the peak of the Iraq war, Canon Andrew White served as rector of St. George's Church, the only Anglican Church in Baghdad. His congregants were some of the last Christians left in the city. In the middle of that war zone, Canon Andrew White was able to offer love and mercy by setting up a free medical clinic for people of all faiths, Muslims and Christians. We were honored to help support and sustain this work.

During that time, Andrew was speaking at a Glory Conference we hosted at our church in Charlotte, North Carolina. The voice of the Lord instructed me to put a large amount of cash into Andrew's coat pocket as I gave him a farewell hug. It was thousands of dollars in cash. Andrew flew directly from our meeting to Baghdad where he was captured by violent kidnappers. Locked in a dark cell, dread and fear creeping upon him, Andrew remembered that the large cash gift we had given him was still in his money belt. Miraculously, Andrew was able to us this gift to ransom himself out of the clutches of that violent terrorist gang.

This book, *The Glory Zone in the War Zone*, is loaded with amazing stories like this that will help take the limits off your faith. From the life of one of the great missionaries in our era, a man I call a true "ambassador of glory," may your eyes be opened to recognize God's presence in every situation.

May a new chapter of signs and wonders be released in your own life as you read this powerful book.

DR. MAHESH CHAVDA
Senior Pastor of All Nations Church
Founder of Chavda Ministries International
Fort Mill, SC

2

CHAPTER ONE

THE GLORY ZONE

For almost two decades I led a vibrant church in Baghdad, the capital of Iraq. During this period, we experienced the brutal reality of war, poverty, bloodshed, torture, terrorism, and extreme hatred. However, we also experienced the glory.

Baghdad was full of zones. The war zone was our home. The green zone was the protected zone and people would queue for hours at checkpoints in order to enter it. The red zone was the "unprotected zone"—it was a zone marked by explosions, bloodshed, and horror, a zone that one would not wish to step in without knowing that one's eternity was protected by the shed blood of Jesus. This was the zone in which all of my congregation at St. George's church lived. The church building was located in Haifa Street, an extremely dangerous location.

Zones were natural to our thinking; in many ways we lived in a "zone mindset." We knew the reality of boundaries, dividing lines, safe and unsafe territory. We knew the dangers of traversing zones and crossing borders; we knew the relief of returning to the green zone—the place of embassy protection.

Living in the reality of this mindset enabled me to gain fresh revelation on the reality of being seated above—the reality of Psalm 91, the secret place or the secret zone. Just as the Embassy chapel was an earthly and spiritual place of governance, peace, and protection, so was the reality for us as citizens of Heaven and ambassadors of Christ.

What is the glory zone? For me it is the place, the domain of His manifest presence. It is the place where we experience the reality of Heaven invading our world, the place where we are tangibly touched by Heaven's realities—transcendent peace, unspeakable joy, angels, visions, extreme light, divine provision, unusual manifestations that reveal an aspect of King Jesus, healings, resurrections, supernatural alignments, divine counsel, miracles, signs, and wonders. It is a zone that becomes increasingly defined, real, and tangible as we move in deep realms of faith, devotion, and worship.

The glory zone is a zone far different from and superior to physically earthly zones that are fixed, static, mapped, and seen. It as an eternal, invisible, dynamic zone that moves with us. The great mystery of "Christ within, the hope of glory" and the great mystery of being "within Him" mean that each of us is designed to abide in this zone and to carry this zone as if it were a transportable tabernacle that can be set up in the darkest of places.

What is interesting to me is the origin of the word *zone*, which comes from the Greek word *zonnumi*, which historically referred to a belt that was worn and to the act of fastening one's garments. Later, *zonnumi* came to refer to a strip of land from where eventually we got the word *zone*. This original meaning speaks to me of *wearing* the zone, *carrying* the zone, and being garmented in it as if were a part of oneself. Many would refer to this as walking in the reality of an open Heaven due to having an intimate relationship with the Father, Son, and Spirit. In the same way that I wore my military body armor, I wore my spiritual armor; I knew that in essence I wore and carried the glory zone. I understood not just the reality of being in His presence but the reality of Him being in my presence. My people and I experienced the tangible, concrete reality of the King's domain (the fullness of His presence) that manifested itself in our midst and followed us just like a shadow. Even in the darkest of hours, we knew the reality of those on the road to Emmaus—the overwhelming awareness of *Him* being in *our* presence and the assurance of being overshadowed by the full presence of the Godhead.

It was only after God gave me this title, *Glory Zone*, that I realized that David Herzog's ministry is actually named Glory Zone and that Patricia King in her Glory School describes a spiritual reality of abiding in the King's presence as the "Throne Zone." This to me is a wonderful description of this realm for there is a King of Glory on the throne; it is the King of Glory's Zone—that is to say, to experience divine glory is to experience the royal, sovereign domain—the *kingdom*.

In the Old Testament the main words used for "glory" are *kabod* and *hod*. The word *hod* is seen as representing majesty, splendor, light, and glory, while *kabod* relates to weight or heaviness. The broader meaning of *kabod* relates to honor or glory, and as we know from John's revelatory vision these are powerful attributes of God's majesty that coexist. Those who lay down their crowns before the throne of Heaven declare:

> *Worthy are You, our Lord and our God, to receive glory and honor and power; for You created all things, and because of Your will they existed, and were created* (Revelation 4:11).

Let us also consider the word *shekinah*, which is not a biblical term but one that was used by post-biblical rabbis and actually allows us to enhance our understanding of *kabod*. The word *shekinah* is derived from the verb *shachan,* which means "to settle, inhabit, or dwell." That is to say, the tangible weight and the radiant light of the glory is something that must be accommodated, housed, or carried. It relates to a continual "dwelling in the midst of" a people or indeed an individual person (as facilitated by the outpouring of the Holy Spirit). In his book *Zechariah and Jewish Renewal*, Fred P. Miller indicates that the prophet Isaiah comes the closest to using the word *shekinah* when he declares:

> *Thus says the high and exalted One who lives forever, whose name is Holy, "I dwell* [shachan] *on a high and holy place, and also with the contrite and lowly of spirit in order to revive the spirit of the lowly and to revive the heart of the contrite"* (Isaiah 57:15).

We will see more clearly as we journey through this book that the glory relates to the "dwelling" presence of God. At times it is visibly seen; at times, though present, it is not seen. As Paul states, we were created to be carriers of the glory and to be the dwelling place where Christ who Himself contains the fullness of the Deity may be fully formed and fully released.

> *Or do you not know that your body is a temple of the Holy Spirit who is in you, whom you have from God, and that you are not your own? For you have been bought with a price: therefore, glorify God in your body* (1 Corinthians 6:19-20).

Furthermore, God wants this glory to be showcased and exhibited across the entire cosmos so that darkness is dispelled and all mankind encounters His majesty. As the light of His glory radiates, the knowledge of this glory will become truly global. The truth of His name will be made known and every knee will bow—for revelation of truth always leads to worship.

> *Let your light shine* [luminous radiance] *before men in such a way that they may see your good works, and glorify your Father who is in heaven* (Matthew 5:16).

The ministry of Jesus is the ministry of light. He is the light of the world, far brighter than all other created lights. He is the very essence of radiance and luminosity, and Heaven requires no other light. This blazing, all-consuming light emanating from His being is the essence of His glory and His kingdom is a kingdom of light. The glory is thus not theoretical; it is experiential. So much of it relates to the realm of seeing and watching the invisible become visible. I most certainly could not have survived in my work without the true experience of the illuminating, overwhelming presence of

Father, Son, and Holy Spirit in my life. Miracles, signs, and wonders are neither fashionable terms nor ancient phenomena. The miracle realm is the *now* realm; it is the eternal realm and it is a realm of deep, radical transforming divine activity, and this was the realm that marked so much of my time in Iraq.

I visited Iraq regularly in the late 1990s during the early years of my ministry several years before the war began. During these initial visits there was always a climate of great tension and unrest in the nation and a sense that civil conflict could erupt and explode at any moment. For Christian Iraqis, one of the most significant annual fasts is a three-day fast referred to as "the fast of Jonah"— the main focus being on divine mercy and national restoration. Nineveh, the city to which Jonah was sent to preach, is located north of Bagdad, just before Iraq turns into Kurdistan. To this day, Nineveh is the only predominantly Christian city in Iraq, and the shrine of Jonah (eventually destroyed by ISIS) is seen by Iraqi Christians as a symbol of obedience and mercy, which form part of their heritage.

As scripture describes, Assyria (modern-day Iraq) committed terrible atrocities and greatly afflicted and oppressed the people of Israel, yet God saw to it that through the prophetic oracle of Jonah (meaning "dove") a gateway would be established through which His mercy, love, and forgiveness could be released. The repentant Ninevites grew into a radical community, devoted to God, and centuries later when Thomas came to Nineveh, he found a strong believing community in place. This community had held fast to the Abrahamic tradition, and thus Jonah's seeds of obedience were seen to have reaped a harvest. When Thomas arrived in Nineveh after the time of Christ, he taught about the life, death, and resurrection of

Jesus the Messiah, and consequently the first Christian community in Mesopotamia (modern-day Iraq) was birthed. This is why many Christian believers in Iraq are still referred to as Assyrians. During my time mediating on the history of the land and on the call to forgive the vilest of enemies, God spoke to me about the unfathomable depths of His mercy and the divine flow of radical forgiveness and virtue that had once watered the soil of this land.

Despite most of our church congregation being Baghdadi, they would all consider Nineveh their traditional home and would nearly all return there during breaks. Many had family and homes there and considered Nineveh as both their familial and spiritual homeland. This is also why so many Christians quickly returned there when radical terrorist groups moved into Baghdad.

Before the terror started in Iraq, there were various attempts to create unity amongst the believers from different traditions within Iraq; however, these endeavors were largely unsuccessful. Yet when the horrors of ISIS took place this was not the case, for in the midst of crisis there was a radical move toward harmony and solidarity. In fragmentation, disunity, rivalry, and division, the revelation of Jesus can never be present in fullness; however, when diverse groups come together as one and where mutual honor presides, Jesus can truly dwell in their midst and the bond of love and peace can truly grow. Where there is a resting place for the Holy Spirit—either an individual or corporate place that is in harmony with Heaven— and where there is divine love, there will always be divine unity. This is why the apostle Paul implores the Ephesians to:

> *Walk in a manner worthy of the calling with*
> *which you have been called, with all humility and*

gentleness, with patience, showing tolerance for one another in love, being diligent to preserve the unity of the Spirit in the bond of peace. There is one body and one Spirit, just as also you were called in one hope of your calling; one Lord, one faith, one baptism, one God and Father of all who is over all and through all and in all (Ephesians 4:1-6).

As the war intensified and acts of persecution started to be perpetrated, I started to see a radical change of mindset among the Iraqi Christians. No longer did people self-differentiate between traditions and denominations; they were simply Christian believers. The disunity that had prevailed during the climate of moderate civil order was replaced by a fresh revelation and a consequent cherishing of collective identity and, above all, the reality and worth of Jesus. The people began to understand the power of divine light within sinister darkness, the prominence of the Father's role as Sovereign Judge, and the reality of their eternal future with Him. As one of the resounding apostolic exhortations from Paul to the church undergoing brutal Roman persecution states:

Never take your own revenge, beloved, but leave room for the wrath of God, for it is written, "Vengeance is Mine, I will repay," says the Lord (Romans 12:19).

It was the clarity of vision and resolution that arose from this united stance that enabled people to stand as one amidst persecution to truly choose forgiveness. There was a united choice by both young and old to release forgiveness rather than vengeance, retribution, and enmity. This forgiveness was voiced on many occasions across the airwaves and on international television. A wave of loving-kindness and a sense of sincere pardon was released from the depths of people's hearts as they embraced the heart and the ways of Jesus. The Glory Zone became a Mercy Zone.

Reflections

The glory is the light, majesty, and presence of the Trinity. It is not simply another word to describe divine preeminence; it is a person in whom we experience awe and refuge. Jesus Himself contains the fullness of the deity, and He calls us into an experience of mutual indwelling. Christ within you is the hope of glory, and part of that glory is also you hidden in Christ—for He, Himself, *"is the radiance of His* [the Father's] *glory and the exact representation of His nature"* (Heb. 1:3). This is the same radiance that the prophet Habakkuk described:

> *His radiance is like the sunlight; He has rays flashing from His hand, and there is the hiding of His power* (Habakkuk 3:4).

I would like to show you throughout this book how the glory is both a person and a place. To abide in the shelter of the Almighty and to become infused with His light is to reside in the place of His glory. That is to say, the "Shelter of the Almighty" is a person and a place.

The glory that passed before Moses was the radiant goodness of God. That is to say, God's response to Moses when he asked to see His glory was the release of a mighty flow of virtue and goodness toward him. *"I Myself will make all my goodness pass before you"* (Exod. 33:19).

It is normal to associate glory and goodness as they relate to a sense of awe, superlative delight, and abundant provision, but have you considered that mercy is as much a part of God's glory as goodness is? From the setting of the glorious rainbow in the sky and the creation of the golden mercy seat overshadowed by the "cherubim of glory" to the moment of all-sufficient sacrifice at Golgotha, this eternal link between glory and mercy was made visible. The kindness of the Father and His ability to forgive the vilest, most heinous of crimes is an integral part of His glory. The cry of "Father, forgive them" remains a cry that releases the weight of His glory.

Just as goodness and mercy follow us together, so do glory and mercy. In essence His glory is His goodness and His merciful kindness—the outflowing of His nature. David's evidence of this enabled him to proclaim with confident assurance that God's unchanging nature and constant, relentless flow of virtue would pursue him on his path for as long as he had life.

> *Surely goodness and mercy shall follow me all the days of my life, and I will dwell in the house of the Lord for ever* (Psalm 23:6 KJV).

Prayer

Father, I ask that as we journey together through this book You awaken fresh faith and ignite expectation, hope, and awe in the hearts of the readers. I ask that You awaken us afresh to the magnitude of Your great mercy and I ask You for revelation and illumination regarding the wonders of Your glory.

CHAPTER TWO

PROPHETIC INFLUENCES

FROM EARLY CHILDHOOD ONWARD, THERE WERE SEVERAL key prophetic influences that marked my life—by this I mean people who either prophesied directly into my future or whose presence in my life became a part of my own voice.

My mother, who was a worship leader within the Pentecostal movement, was dedicated by the great healing minister Smith Wigglesworth; and her father (my grandfather) was his personal assistant for many years and traveled the world with him.

As a child I was greatly influenced by my mother, and every Thursday, as a ten-year old boy on the way back from school, I would stop at the local Assemblies of God church to listen to my mother sing. The Thursday afternoon prayer meeting started during my last hour at school and finished about thirty minutes after I arrived there at 4 PM. As soon as I arrived, I would go the church kitchen, find a drink and a cookie, and go into the church where all the local women where gathered for their worship meeting. Each week I would sit at the back and absorb the atmosphere; then my mother and I would walk home together, and she would prepare supper. It was during one of these meetings that I met a man named John Carter who had been a student of Smith Wigglesworth and was a close friend of Donald Gee. Mr. Carter once came up to me during one of the women's prayer meetings and told me that, though I was just a young boy, God was going to use me in a great and mighty way. He said to me, "Andrew, one day your name will be known around the world and the call of God on your life is very big." I do not remember every detail but, as a young boy, my childhood impressions led me to hide these the words *big* and *call* in my heart. Sometimes just a few inspiring words from Heaven enable the ground of a child's heart to receive the prophetic seeds of the future.

Beyond the Four Walls

During the mid to late 1980s, a further key prophetic influence in my life shaped my student years. I was highly influenced by the ministry of Pentecostal evangelist and prophetess Mrs. Jean Darnall, who was very active in the UK during that time. Mrs. Darnall was an ordained missionary for the International Church of the Foursquare Gospel and the founder of several Foursquare churches in many nations. She was appointed associate pastor of Angelus Temple, Los Angeles and served there for six years following the death of Aimee Semple McPherson, who had been her pastor and mentor. Jean then went on to be a strong influence upon many traditional churches, including the Anglican Church in Great Britain, during the Charismatic Renewal. During their twenty-five years in England, the Darnalls established a Foursquare church and Bible college and were instrumental in the establishment of "The Festival of Light"—an event that resulted in thousands of young people forming "The March for Jesus" in Britain and worldwide.

In my years as a medical student I attended many of Mrs. Darnall's meetings at St. Mark's, Kennington, the church that I was attending during this time. I became immersed in the prophetic atmospheres of Mrs. Darnall's services and in the rich presence of God and anointed worship that characterized these gatherings. It was in these powerful meetings (along with other revival-based events in 1980s London) that I experienced the tangible nearness of God's presence and the fullness of the glory surrounding me at work.

There was a strong link between St. Mark's church and the Christian Union at St. Thomas' hospital where I was a medical student, and around one hundred other medical students working at the hospital also attended the revival meetings. One of the most extreme miracles that I witnessed in England took place during this time. As part of their training, medical students were involved in observing surgical operations. One patient named Mr. Ray Austin was suffering from inoperable cancer of the bronchus. We observed Mr. Austin undergo thoracic surgery and watched as the surgeons closed him concluding that treatment was not an option and his situation was beyond hope. It was a tragic situation and they give Mr. Austin three weeks to live. However, Mr. Austin was the unsaved husband of a new Christian who believed with all her heart that Jesus could heal him. A few of us thus sought permission from his wife to bring a group from church to St. Thomas' hospital that they may stand with her and gather at his bedside to pray for him. Mr. Ray Austin was totally healed that night, and after a series of biopsies and reexaminations by leading oncologists, he was declared completely cancer-free. Mr. Austin gave his life to Jesus that same night and he and Mrs. Austin later started a vibrant home group. I, among others, attended the Austins' home group and saw several miracles take place there. This whole experience marked my life in a powerful way as I began to experience the extreme redemptive and restorative power of God and the reality of taking the priestly ministry outside the "four walls of the church." Later in my career, I was to experience, in equal measure, the reality of taking medical ministry outside the "four walls of the hospital." I believe there is a lesson here for all of us: Do not self-restrict and self-categorize. The professional you is not separate from the spiritual you. The glory of God inside of you is not limited to the contexts, spaces and parameters that you expect Him to move in. The glory is about "all of Him in all of you."

The senior pastor of St. Mark's was a very godly man named Mr. Nicholas Rivett-Carnac, and he was greatly influential during this time due to his deep hunger to see the Holy Spirit move in great power. During one service when Mrs. Darnall was present, an old, humble Afro-Caribbean man, who I didn't know but who was in regular attendance of the revival meetings, asked, during the service, if he could pray with me. He told me that God had shown him that Israel and the message of Israel would play a central part in my future life. At that time, I had no real grid for this word, no context, and no understanding; I did not know the man, yet I felt deep peace in my spirit as he prayed for me.

My father had always had a great love and affection for the Jewish people and had always taught me to love and pray for Israel; this I did to such an extent that, as a child, I would dress up as a police man and protect the local Jewish cemetery. My parents also welcomed elderly homeless Jews into our home, gave them a bed and a place to rest, cooked for them, and invited local Polish Jews to join us for family picnics in the park. These Polish Jews became "family," and I can still remember them showing us their concentration camp numbers tattooed on their arms from when they had been prisoners in the camps. I listened with horror as my parents educated me regarding the incomprehensible atrocities of the Holocaust and the rationale behind the tattooed camp identification numbers that my young eyes beheld. Aside from these experiences, I had no real grid for Israel and the Jewish people and only later did I start to see how those sweet, heroic, infantile gestures of protecting the Jewish cemetery, housing the homeless, and listening to the traumatized were prophetic acts related to my future. Years later, in addition to engaging in key reconciliation work in Israel, I would find myself acting as a rabbi and refuge to the few remaining Jews of Baghdad.

We must always look back with awe and gratitude at the days of small beginnings. In those early days of childhood, I used to circulate the neighborhood in a little wooden handmade go-cart made by my father designed for me in the shape of a Silver Ghost Rolls Royce. When I wasn't parked at the Jewish cemetery guarding the gates in my policeman's uniform, I was delivering plasters, bandages, and first aid to children who had injured themselves playing in the streets. Again, these were prophetic gestures that spoke of my future as a doctor, a priest, and a protector of the weak.

I trained as an anesthesiologist, as there was always a deep desire in me to reduce and eliminate the pain of others. I then went on to study for a doctorate in the role of Israel in Christian theology and later did a doctorate in Judaism while directing the Cambridge University Society of Jews and Christians and chairing the young leadership section of the International Council of Christians and Jews. I am sure that all of us can look back in a similar way and see how the seeds of future commissioning were already planted, cultivated, and nurtured in our early years of development. God often prepares us in our youth for the divine pathways of our future.

Legacy of Faith

It was in the year of 1998 just before my grandfather's graduation to Heaven that he passed on to me the Bible of Smith Wigglesworth. This Bible, which is filled with Wigglesworth's private notes, traveled with me all over the world and still does. During my darkest moments in Baghdad, the great power of the scriptures, as testified by the man of faith who held them, enabled me to sustain my own faith in the miraculous and to reach to God for the impossible and the irrational. I had been taught by one of my mentors, Donald Coggan, a former Archbishop of Canterbury, to be a faith-filled risk-taker. He taught me that faith and prudence do not work against each other as both are attributes of the Holy Spirit. He instilled in me the importance of dreaming big, abandoning the rational, and stepping into God's unlimited capacity to act on man's behalf.

> Put this right in your mind and never forget it: you will never be of any importance to God till you venture into the impossible. God wants people on the daring line. I do not mean foolish daring. *Be filled*

with the Spirit" (Ephesians 5:18b), and when we are filled with the Spirit, we are not so much concerned about the secondary thing. It is the first with God.[1]

My hunger for the anointing and for the manifest presence of Jesus grew stronger as I reflected on the great legacy of faith that had so influenced my own family line. When I read Smith's notes and the scriptures that he highlighted so meticulously, I am drawn to meditate on them afresh and allow God to bring new revelation to me as I carry my own cross.

A very close friend of mine is Dr. Henry Fardell, the great-grand-son of Smith Wigglesworth. Dr. Fardell had been raised in the Elim Pentecostal church and amidst the many connections that we shared (including the fact that he became my dentist!), his love for the Jewish people and his links with Iraqi dentists were an important part of our relationship. The story is too long to tell here, but meeting him was one of several great divinely orchestrated friend-ships that have enriched my life and work. I was recently with his sons and grandsons talking with them about their heritage and discussing with Dr. Fardell the powerful moves of God that his great-grandfather released and saw prophetically for the genera-tions ahead of him. His life and his passion have left a deep legacy in England and across the world and his faith for the impossible continues to inspire me on so many levels.

Ms. Ruth Ward Heflin

I experienced another great prophetic voice who spoke into my life in 1988 during my doctoral studies at the Hebrew University of Jerusalem and at an Orthodox Jewish *yeshiva* (university). It was during this time that my rabbi, Rabbi Naphtali, advised me to attend a meeting with a lady whose name I had never heard. The speaker was called Ms. Ruth Ward Heflin, and she was known in Jerusalem for being a great lover of God and a person who moved in great power. I was somewhat bemused and astonished by his advice as, first, this was an orthodox rabbi advising me to go to a highly unconventional, dynamic, vibrant Christian gathering; second, the one to whom he was directing me was a *woman!* Moreover, the woman in question was a person whom neither of us knew and whose credibility neither of us could even begin to vouch for. He explained to me that there was a group of Christians known as the Mount Zion Fellowship. People gathered in the neighborhood of Sheikh Jarrah in a residence on Ragheb Nashashibi Street in the (predominantly Arab) east side of Jerusalem. He said there was a large house gathering every Saturday evening and great miracles and "spiritual happenings" were being reported. What he meant, in our New Testament language, was that there was a great outpouring of the Holy Spirit.

Intrigued and curious as to what exactly my rabbi was referring to, I attended the gathering that Saturday evening. The worship was deep, radical, heavenly, and as Ms. Heflin led the worship there was such an overwhelming holy presence; it was like nothing I had experienced before. At the end of the meeting Ms. Heflin gave out mini Mars bars and Snickers bars and we had these with a cup of tea. I thought it was a great service of spiritual and physical feasting, and as I ate my chocolate she approached me and pointed at me, shouting to get my attention. Then, without saying anything else or asking my name, she placed her hand on my head and began to prophesy the call of God on my life to work for peace in the Middle East. These were her exact words that I recorded:

> Young man, while Jerusalem will never be your home, you will come and go from this city with a divine mission. The hand of God has been placed upon you for a divine work in this region and you will be a carrier of God's peace in the Middle East during a desperate time.

The great significance of this event was threefold: God showed me how he could use an orthodox rabbi to lead me straight into an atmosphere of His glory and that there are times in our lives when scrolls of destiny must be collected, read, and received. Second, my experience of the Holy Spirit and the manifest presence of Jesus in Ms. Heflin's meetings transported me into a whole new world and marked the start of a beautiful lifelong friendship with this great prophetess who shared my deep love for Jerusalem and for the Jewish people. My orthodox rabbi, Rabbi Naphtali, esteems himself honored to still have Ms. Heflin's piano in his home in Meir Sherim. Third, the prophecy given by Ms. Heflin became crucial within the outworking of God's plan in and through my life.

I believe for all of us there are those *kairos* moments, those great "suddenlys" of God, divine windows of change where life-transforming prophetic downloads are given. It is so important that we tune to the flow of Holy Spirit and receive His words with open hearts without attempting to rationalize the words that we hear. I say this because my natural mind wanted to receive this word as a call exclusively to Jerusalem, the place of my passion; however, God had different plans, and in the fullness of time I learned that the Middle East was bigger than Jerusalem.

Dr. Billy Graham

A further great influence on my life was the late Dr. Billy Graham. Dr. Graham was highly instrumental in my ministry during the late 1990s. He assisted me greatly in facilitating meetings and dialogues aimed at finding a way toward civil peace and reconciliation. The crisis in Iraq had been one of Dr. Graham's key concerns and the plight of Iraqi Christians was close to his heart. We became very good friends and he assisted me greatly by hosting a meeting in the US with the Iraqi delegation from the Iraqi government, which consisted of three of the nation's most senior religious leaders. During this period of time spent with Dr. Graham, I found myself constantly moved by his sincerity, humility, and faith. We discussed a lot together and I always sensed a deep purity and holiness in his approach to issues big and small. He was a gracious and attentive listener, earnest and compassionate in his desire to support the leaders in their quest to find a solution. I learned so much from Dr. Graham and his dear wife Ruth, especially during the peak of my ministry in the Middle East. Above all, I received a whole new level of revelation regarding the true meaning of unconditional love and gained insights into the radical power of the cross that I have never received from anyone else.

Dr. Graham later invited me to speak and lecture at his college, Wheaton College, and I have been a friend of Wheaton ever since. It has been a real honor to be have been so involved with teaching and ministering to the students there and to see the rich legacy that Dr. Graham has left to the next generation.

How do we respond to prophetic words and prophetic inspiration? As I look back on my life, I would say there are three fundamental keys to our response. First, we must listen attentively and wait for the witness of the Holy Spirit in our hearts. Prophecy is spiritual, not intellectual; thus, we must always wait for the deep, peaceful witness of the Holy Spirit. Second, we must check that the word does not contravene the nature or ways of God and that it aligns fully with biblical truth. Third, we must posture ourselves in a position to receive the fulfilment of the word. This involves taking ownership of it, embracing it, agreeing with it, declaring it, cooperating with it, and asking God to confirm and illuminate it. Like Mary our prayer must be, "Let it be done unto me according to thy word."

Reflections

Prophetic words and influences are to be cherished and honored. We must be quick to recognize and thank God for those whose presence in our personal lives has laid the foundations of our faith. Yet we must remember that Jesus Himself was and is the greatest prophet. He is Prophet, Priest, and King. Jesus was the greatest living and divine oracle (the Word incarnate), the greatest seer (He did only that which He saw His Father do), the greatest foreteller, and the greatest forthteller. In Luke 4:24 when Jesus states that *"no prophet is welcome in his hometown,"* He was clearly referring to the ministry of His own prophetic voice.

Within the throne room of Heaven, the testimony of Jesus' blood, His all-sufficient sacrifice, and His priestly reign is itself the Spirit of prophecy. His words over you right now as you read this are good and true, they are redemptive words of life and love, He intercedes for you, and His blood is on the mercy seat. If you have never received a prophetic word or do not recognize a prophetic influence that has marked your life, rest assured that if you have received and embraced the voice and influence of Jesus then you have received the greatest of all prophets. His words over you, whether stated in scripture or whispered in your ear, are the most powerful, unshakable words that you can receive.

Prayer

Father, I ask that as the reader journeys through this book You minister to them prophetically that they may receive divine inspiration and guidance from You. I bless them with all that You would say to them, Spirit of Truth, and I ask that Your voice resounds deeply within their hearts.

Note

1. Smith Wigglesworth, edited by Wayne Warner, *The Anointing of His Spirit* (Bloomington, MN: Chosen Books, 1994), 47.

CHAPTER THREE

THE GLORY IN THE BETHLEHEM SIEGE

You have ascended on high, You
have led captivity captive.
—PSALM 68:18 NKJV

MY FIRST DRAMATIC EXPERIENCE OF THE GLORY IN THE WAR zone was in April 2002 when I mediated negotiations in the Middle East during a very serious period of conflict known as the Bethlehem Siege. The Israeli Defense Force had launched a major ground and air attack on Bethlehem and fighting broke out in the streets in Manger Square as Israeli soldiers instigated an extensive search for dangerous Palestinian militants. Approximately two hundred Palestinians fleeing Israeli troops had broken into the compound around the Church of the Nativity. Over sixty priests, monks, and nuns who lived in this compound were trapped inside with Palestinian civilians and gunmen amongst whom there were several heavily armed militia members. The militants had sought refuge in the square near the church assuming that Israel would not fight within such proximity to a Christian holy site. This fourth-century church was built over the site that Christians had identified as being the place of the birth of Jesus.

I was close friends with the then-deputy foreign minister of Israel, Rabbi Michael Melchior, and I received a series of urgent calls from him, Yasser Arafat, and the Archbishop of Canterbury, George Carey, to return to Bethlehem and mediate negotiations. On arriving in Bethlehem, I realized how horrific things were. A military operation known as Defensive Shield was underway in the West Bank and a significant amount of the territory was under siege.

At first, the trapped Palestinians ate food stored by the monks and nuns who live there; but as time progressed from days into weeks, conditions seriously deteriorated—food and water had run out and all but one line of electricity was cut off.

There had been deaths inside the church compound, and the innocent civilians held inside were suffering from dehydration and unable to negotiate with their besiegers. The atmosphere in Bethlehem was dark, menacing, sinister, and full of fear.

The streets were packed with Israeli tanks, military trucks and burnt-out cars. Palestinian fighters had been forcing their way into homes and firing a constant stream of rockets and mortar shells into Beit Jala—a neighboring town that was largely Christian. Israel had responded by sending Apache helicopters to destroy the homes from which the missiles were being fired and, as is so often the case, the Christians found themselves trapped in the middle of a horrific war zone.

I spent long days in intense discussions with politicians; Christian, Jewish, and Muslim leaders; and a significant amount of time and energy trying to get food to help the people in Bethlehem and the neighbouring towns of Beit Jala and Beit Sahour. We were faced with a huge humanitarian crisis especially in regard to those living near the church. The curfew was only lifted for three hours every two or three days and even when it was lifted, many people were scared to go out and find food. Consequently, we were constantly trying to prepare large bags of food and deliver them to all those in need as well as to a group of Ethiopian monks living in Manger Square who had nothing to eat or drink.

It was in this climate of desperation, amidst the sound of gunfire and explosions, that I received further news regarding the plight of an older man named Edmond Nasser who had recently returned home from the hospital following open-heart surgery and was in a serious condition due to not being able to access the medication required for his recovery. Edmond and his wife lived on the edge of Manger Square in the center of Bethlehem, which was cut off, and the British consulate who knew of my previous medical training had advised them to contact me. I knew when I received the call that God was calling me to rise up and act in His divine strength and would somehow enable me to get to Edmond despite it seeming impossible.

I contacted the local Israeli commander, Shmueli Hamburger, who was a colonel in the reservists and who worked with the Israeli Ministry of Religious Affairs with oversight of the Christian communities and occupied territories. I passed on the message from the British Consulate and asked him to get me into the city urgently as a man was dying. His response was that it was "far too dangerous" and that I would be "seriously risking my life." Nevertheless, the voice of God was resonating so deeply with me and I knew that I had to get to this man.

My Israeli driver who knew the area well found a back route into Beit Jala, and we went as far as we could before quickly leaving the car to climb over some rocky barren land in order to get nearer to our destination. This was no easy task as from the place where we had to leave the car, we still had another two miles to go and I was absolutely exhausted. The courage and the boldness were there but it was exhausting. As I stood tired and weary with my medical bag in my hand and my head raised to Heaven asking my Father for divine assistance, I felt faith rise and experienced a wave of deep peace wash over me. As this happened, a man who had the appearance of a local man suddenly appeared from nowhere. I am still convinced that this man was an angel. He came running toward us, and when I asked him his name, he said Mustafa (which in Arabic means "chosen one"). This man did not look like an angel in the way that I have seen angels since—he was a normal-looking person dressed in normal clothes—however, he carried a unique presence. Even though his name was Arabic and he appeared to be local, his car had Israeli plates on, which was unusual. As he asked us where we wanted to go, I felt another strange peace flood my being—the same tangible peace as I had felt consume me the moment before he arrived. The man drove us at an extremely high speed to the Beit Jala King Hussein hospital where we met with

Colonel Hamburger who we then followed to the home of Mr. Nasser.

Upon arrival I was able to dress Mr. Nasser's wounds, give him the medication that he required, and pray with him and his wife. He made a successful recovery and lived on for several more years. As we left Edmond's house, Colonel Hamburger instructed our mysterious driver, Mustafa, to follow his own vehicle very slowly through the city and not to take any other route. However, with no conversation, warning, or explanation, Mustafa ignored all military instructions, hit the accelerator, and sped away as soon as we entered the car. I ought to have felt terrified, yet the strange sense of peace continued despite the high-speed journey, which was full of radical swerves. I felt very much as if I were on a race-car track.

As our car arrived from our "alternative" route at the District Command Office, Colonel Hamburger ran to Mustafa's vehicle and greeted us with anxious trembling and tears of relief. On returning from Edmond's house, someone had thrown a bomb directly at his vehicle which landed and exploded just behind it. If we had heeded his instruction and followed his car, we would have been caught in the explosion and killed outright.

I have reflected on this event a lot over the years and I am still convinced within my spirit that this mysterious (almost silent) driver named Mustafa was an angel who, in accordance with the meaning of his name, had been commissioned to assist us. He had appeared seemingly from nowhere, did not charge us a fee, and he disappeared at a speed. Furthermore, during the thirty-nine days of the siege there were no other vehicles or taxis allowed in the town, so his presence there was a mystery. The only people on the streets outside of the short curfew hours were the army and me. This mysterious man had been peaceful, serene, and fearless and seemed to have carried a unique knowledge and intuition of what was happening—that is to say, he had a level of awareness, insight, and aptitude superior to the earthly knowledge and wisdom of the military. It seemed that he had been assigned to us for the specific task of entering the danger zone, reaching Mr. Nasser, and ministering to him. Though without uniform, he appeared to be a man of superior rank to the military colonel whose orders he ignored. His level of skill, insight, authority, kindness, and aptitude was simply not normal. Due to my position, I personally had been and continued to be a very familiar face in Bethlehem; I knew many families well, as well as drivers and assistants, yet I had never once seen this man before and I never once saw him since. When I inquired as to who he might be, no one knew. To this day, I do not understand what happened, but what I do know is that on that day, I experienced the overwhelming presence of the Prince of Peace and the full backing of Heaven as I undertook one of the most dangerous of tasks.

As I returned to the scene of conflict, I could see that tensions were steadily intensifying. A group of Franciscan monks had decided to remain in the Church of the Nativity compound as voluntary hostages in order to show solidarity to the Palestinians and reduce bloodshed while many of the Palestinian civilians who were trapped inside were experiencing a double siege as they were fearful to come out onto the streets even if they could, lest they be blown up or fired at by the army. The decaying bodies of men who had been shot inside were eventually carried out on makeshift coffins while dehydrating people trapped in the siege had been reduced to using water from the well to boil lemon leaves from the lemon trees that grew in the courtyard.

The Palestinian negotiating team attempted to exchange food for the release of civilians held in the church; however, the gunmen refused to accept the offer and the thirty-nine-day period of mediating negotiations that followed remained tedious, exhausting, and seemingly impossible. Yet within all of the turmoil and frustration, I could feel God's glory rising in and on me. I remember one night, when we were right in the heart of crucial negotiations, I returned to my base in Jerusalem at the Mount Zion hotel, and as I began to sing in the spirit alone in my room and pray for divine acceleration, redemption of the captives, and a solution to be released I became covered in gold and silver. This was the only time I have had gold and silver land all over me at the same time. In fact, only very rarely have I seen supernatural silver appear as most often it has been gold. The suit that I was still wearing was literally covered in gold and silver, and when I looked in the mirror, my face and hair were covered in this dazzling glitter. This was a great sign to me of God's glory and Him releasing His "ownership" of Bethlehem, His possession.

As I looked at myself glittering in the mirror, my mind turned to Haggai 2:8: *"The silver is Mine, and the gold is Mine,"* and the burden of frustration instantly lifted from me as I felt God's hand of ownership and intervention being released. I felt energy and joy fill my body and began to see light at the end of the tunnel as I knew that silver represented redemption and that God's redemptive activity was being released. Clarity would be provided in the midst of confusion and strife. Right there in my hotel room as I stepped beyond physical exhaustion and into a place of intimacy with God, I was experiencing the glory zone within the war zone.

During the next few days, the Israeli prime minister, Ariel Sharon, stated that the trapped gunmen had a choice of either facing trial in Israel or accepting permanent exile; however, the Palestinians refused to agree. The seemingly endless stream of inconclusive meetings thus continued, and then on day thirty-nine the great breakthrough that I knew I had been promised finally arrived. The Palestinian Authority and the Israeli Defense Force agreed to release the terrorists from the church and send certain men to Gaza and others abroad. The suddenness of this agreement was itself a miracle; it was an abrupt interruption to a long series of scenarios that had made any form of solution increasingly impossible. During the morning of day forty, on arriving at the airport to return to my family, I received messages from church leaders and intercessory groups literally all over the globe. They had been praying fervently during each day of the siege for God's glory to cover me, for divine wisdom, angelic assistance, and supernatural protection to be released to me and for the liberation of all those held captive. We must never underestimate the prayers of the saints.

It was only after the siege days that I began to see how the inner fortitude and reliance on God that I had experienced in this time of crisis was preparing me for life and victory in the war zones of Baghdad. During those early years of diplomatic work in Israel, I had no idea that my future would be spent in Iraq, but God did. It was my involvement in the Bethlehem siege that marked and shaped the ministry I was to fulfil. This difficult thirty-nine days established and illuminated my calling, exposed the need to step confidentially into divine strength, and sensitized me to a new dimension of God.

As the siege was drawing to an end, I was reflecting on the miraculous protection of life that so many families had experienced despite having their homes destroyed. Within one single week, one of my beloved families had seen the sudden birth of over thirty tortoises in the garden. The father of this family is a close friend of mine named Joseph and he is a carpenter by trade. Joseph is a very God-fearing man, and during the siege he had spent each day in fervent prayer. The sudden birth of the tortoises in the garden had taken place as liberation drew near and they became a great sign to all of us. Never had such an unprecedented number of tortoises appeared in a garden within one week. People were astonished and neighbors would go in to witness and photograph the sight. These multiple tortoise births signified the divine physical protection that God had granted us during the siege. Though we had no body armor like the tortoise, we had a naturally supernatural shell of protection and refuge, a transportable "hiding place." The mysterious tortoise births also signified multiplication and longevity as tortoises have one of the longest lifespans in the animal world. I believe that their birth was a prophetic sign not just of the preservation of human life but of the protection of God's purposes for His people in Bethlehem, the longevity and endurance of their faith, and the multiplication of the harvest in the region. As God had redeemed Bethlehem from the hands of terror, so He would see to it that the work He had begun in His people would be brought to completion and passed on from generation to generation.

Throughout the period of rebuilding that took place after the end of the siege and during the Intifada that followed a few years later, Joseph the carpenter and I had regular experiences with angels. In many instances the angels appeared as visible walls of radiant light, and one would often feel a sudden wind, breeze, or electrical charge. They always emerged during times of great danger. On one such occasion, I was standing on the roof of a newly acquired building in Beit Jala where we were just about to start a school for the Aramaic-speaking Christians, when a missile flew past me and missed my leg by literally two feet. (As I mentioned, these were before the days of my having military body armor in Iraq.) As the missile passed beyond me, I could feel myself enwrapped by a holy presence, and I knew that I was being protected and surrounded by angelic majesties.

The school building on which I was standing that day was developed—and just last year, I was at the graduation of the first generation of those who had been toddlers during the siege. They spoke at their graduation of how their families had been raised from the ashes and how their lives had been marked by God's faithfulness and divine favor. These young ones are living oracles and their parents have not allowed them to forget or discard the stories and testimonies of their ancient and familial heritage. They have not forgotten their Creator or Redeemer in the days of their youth, and they are the true heroes of Bethlehem. Many of these "children of the siege" are now at universities in Israel and in different nations. They carry a deep and sincere love and reverence for God and my continuous prayer is that they will remain radical lovers of Jesus and audacious and anointed liberators who know and release God's glory in the days ahead.

This small town of Bethlehem—"the House of Bread" and the dwelling of kings, the place where David and Ruth experienced the depths of the living God, the home of the sacred well (physical and spiritual) from which David craved water, the birthplace of the Bread of all Life, the town whose soil is marked by blood, infanticide, and glory—remains a place where the lamp of the Lord has most assuredly not been extinguished. Praise and worship continue to arise from the Christian minority that remains, and a radiant light shines forth within the darkness. In this humble town invaded throughout the centuries by Muslim armies, Crusaders, and Ottomans, on this soil marked by bloody massacre and intense glory, households of light remain united in their adoration of King Jesus. These are households who, though few in number, have taken their stand for righteousness, love, and truth.

Reflections

Sieges are mentioned frequently throughout Israel's history and referred to throughout the Old Testament. A siege is a military blockade of a city or fortress with the intent of conquering by sustained attack or a well-prepared assault. A siege occurs when an attacker encounters a city or fortress that cannot be easily taken by a quick assault and which refuses to surrender. Thick walls and gates of ancient cities enabled the ancient watchmen to resist besiegers. The Hebrew word for *siege* is *mâtsôwr*, which translates as a "hemming in."

Similarly, on a spiritual level sieges, blockades, and the feeling of being "hemmed in" can take multiple forms. The feeling of being hijacked, sabotaged, invaded, surrounded by adversarial forces, and trapped by the enemy takes place within relationships, finances, careers, and within so many experiences of life. It may even be that you experience a siege in your body or that at night you find yourself besieged by nightmares.

As I experienced in Bethlehem, sieges can be exhausting and long, yet God truly does enable us to withstand. He is our strength, our fortress, and our great liberator. Like David we must stand firm and hold fast to the knowledge of who He is: *"The Lord has become my fortress"* (Ps. 94:22 NIV).

Rest assured that during times of siege, God is still present, His glory and His life-giving joy are still available to you, and His angels are active. He is still on the throne. It was during the siege that the Holy Spirit surrounded me and imparted wisdom, might, and counsel that enabled me to persist even when things seemed impossible. As my good friend Michael W. Smith sings in a recent song: "It may look like I'm surrounded but I'm surrounded by You."[1] This must be your anthem in times of crisis and besiegement.

Prayer

Father, I lift up to You every reader and each family represented. For those who feel besieged in their bodies, relationships, workplaces, finances, or communities, I ask that You move powerfully upon them, release Your angels in their midst and bring divine liberation and deliverance. As they abide in Your presence, release overwhelming joy and let Your promise that "those whom the Son sets free are free indeed" have its full effect in every home.

Note

1. Elyssa Smith, "Surrounded (Fight My Battles)," UPPERROOM Worship team, Dallas, TX; recorded by Michael W. Smith, *World's Favourite New Worship Songs*, Rocketown Records/The Fuel Music, 2017.

CHAPTER FOUR

RADICAL DIVINE REVERSAL

UNDERSTANDING THAT THE PURPOSES OF GOD ARE ALWAYS restorative and redemptive enables us to have a greater anticipation for the radical reversals of God to take place. Throughout scripture we see two common principles that are in fact foundational principles of the kingdom. These are *reversal* and *exchange*. When curses are broken and circumstances reversed, we see the bestowal of blessing and the establishment of the kingdom in its place. The culmination of this is seen at Calvary when the curse was reversed, death was revoked, and the great exchange took place. Death for Life, sorrow for joy, despair for hope, captivity for freedom, dispossession for repossession.

> *The Spirit of the Lord God is upon me, because the Lord has anointed me to bring **good news to the afflicted**; he has sent me to **bind up the***

*brokenhearted, to proclaim **liberty to captives** and **freedom to prisoners;** to proclaim the favorable year of the Lord and the day of vengeance of our God; **to comfort all who mourn,** to grant those who mourn in Zion, **giving them a garland instead of ashes, the oil of gladness instead of mourning, the mantle of praise instead of a spirit of fainting.** So they will be called oaks of righteousness, the planting of the Lord, that He may be glorified* (Isaiah 61:1-3).

God never removes without reestablishing; the system of divine exchange is central to His kingdom—He never dethrones without enthroning Himself. Where His people are, His domain is. We are called to be territorial; we are called to be ground-takers, stewards of divine exchange. We are called to be God's redeemers and restorers, those who stand in the gap and reverse the tide of darkness by standing together as a tsunami wave of light.

A significant part of my time in Baghdad involved seeing the reality and depth of this great truth and watching Heaven move on our behalf in a most extraordinary way. The only Anglican church building in Baghdad had been in a state of serious dilapidation and disrepair. Most of its contents had been stripped, stolen, or destroyed during the war and the place was derelict. The first gathering consisted of around fifty military personnel and the building was surrounded by tanks with helicopters hovering overhead. Within the all of the chaos and tumult I heard God tell me to declare Haggai 2:9: "*'The latter glory of this house will be greater than the former,' says the Lord of hosts, 'and in this place I will give peace*,'" and I knew that God was going to do a great work in our midst.

After the arrest of Saddam Hussein, his swimming pool became the pool for the coalition Provisional Authority. It was a large outdoor pool with blue marble tiles; on each tile was imprinted the dictator's initials "SH" and often the imprints were in gold. However, God was about to replace the tyrant's signature with His own as this very pool also became our embassy chapel baptistry. After the removal of Saddam Hussein, several of those baptized in his pool were key members of the coalition forces. Some of the very first to be baptized were soldiers from the Korean army who had made a decision to follow Jesus. On the first morning of baptisms we had a whole group of unrelated Koreans getting baptized— General Kim, Brigadier Kim, Colonel Kim, and Captain Kim. I remember praying in my room on the previous night about what we should sing at the baptisms and welling up from heart was that old song "Because He lives, I can face tomorrow." We sang this around the pool at the top of our voices. All of my worship team there at the poolside with their instruments were all ex-Wheaton College military men who had been former students of mine at Wheaton and had been young cadets when I was there. Little did we know that we would all be reunited there in a war zone, declaring the salvation of our King around the former pool of one of the most heinous dictators in modern history.

The presence of God was tangible in our midst, and as we gathered to baptize and worship, there was such a deep presence of the Holy Spirit. It was just three months later that, while lecturing in Wheaton College, Chicago, I received a phone call from Gloria Gaither, the writer of "Because He Lives," inviting me to their home. As I sat in the home of the Gaithers, I felt overwhelmed by the love of God in them and humbled to be in the presence of the songwriters whose lyrics became one of our greatest signature songs during the years of war and bloodshed.

The Republican palace was a huge palace with large, spacious rooms in the shape of a semicircle and gigantic bronze statues of Saddam's head and shoulders on its four corners. There was a lot of gold inside; even the taps were made of gold, and many objects, including cutlery, all bore his seal, crest, and initials. However, as with the pool, God had superior plans for this palace, and it became the US embassy chapel while Saddam's throne of solid gold became a very comfortable pulpit for which I was most grateful. God was dismantling the powers of evil and progressively de-territorializing the enemy before our eyes. He was shifting the wealth of the rich tyrant into the governance and jurisdiction of His people. Behind my pulpit there remained the former painted pictures of scud missiles, a telling backdrop that during our worship spoke of glory amidst darkness, life and reconciliation amidst war and dereliction, light amidst darkness.

Near the palace stood the former brothel of Saddam's sons. This had been converted into a small but comfortable residence that housed me and my associates for a three-month period before we moved to live within the US military compound. The residence was small but smart—velvet curtains, large satin cushions, and several baths. It was located in "little Venice" very close to the palace, a place named according to its streams and bridges. It was a protected place under high security, and we benefited accordingly. Again, this is a powerful picture of our call to occupy enemy territory. That which had once been a house of perversion and darkness become a house of prayer and light.

On one memorable evening, Dr. Mowaffak Al Rubaie, the National Security Advisor to the whole of Iraq, asked me if he could use my fountain pen as he had decided that mine was the best fountain pen in Baghdad. Dr. Mowaffak Al Rubaie was a man whom I trusted; he had formerly been known in England as Dr. Baker and he was one of the consultant physicians with whom I had worked during my medical days. I had no idea why he wished to borrow my pen. It was an expensive Pelican fountain pen, my favorite German make of pen, and it had been given to me as a gift. As the official ink color within the political spheres and echelons of Iraq was a dark green, my pen was full of dark green ink, and though this particular pen was precious to me I did not wish to decline Dr. Mowaffak's request to borrow it especially as he explained to me that Prime Minister Nouri Al-Maliki himself had asked to use it. I had no idea why the Prime Minister would wish to borrow my pen, but I obliged him and hoped that he would return the pen to me after using it. Well so it was that night as I switched on the Iraqi news (Al Baghdadi TV) to see the latest headlines, there before my eyes was the Prime Minister using my Pelican fountain pen to sign the death sentence of Saddam Hussein. The evil oppressor whose pool had become my baptistry, whose palace had become my chapel, and whose throne had become my pulpit was now being sentenced to death before the eyes of the world with the ink of my personal fountain pen. This pen that signed the death sentence of a tyrant was thankfully returned to me and it continues to write "life sentences" as I use it to sign Bibles, books, baptism cards, baby dedication cards, graduation certificates, and wedding cards on my travels all over the world.

We must pause and ask ourselves: What type of God could turn a dilapidated empty church building—whose only sign of life was a few trapped pigeons—into the home of 6,500 worshipers? What type of God is so alive in His people that amidst bloodshed and torture they are described by journalists and ambassadors as the "most joy-filled congregation they have ever visited"? What type of God could grant me sufficient courage to attend a sinister dinner party under compulsion with the sons of Saddam—two of the most evil leaders I have met? What type of God could, within a day, take the royal emblems of a tyrant and turn them into a house of prayer and worship? What kind of God could enable me to provide spiritual care to thousands upon thousands of Iraqis and offer tons of food and resources to Christians and Muslims alike? What type of God could enable me to provide within my own "territory" a mini-synagogue and place of shelter for terrorized Jews?

I will tell you exactly what type of God this is. This is the God of Abraham, Isaac, and Jacob, the great sovereign covenant-keeper, the God of divine reversal, the redeemer-restorer, the God of the great exchange, the God who tears down rulers from their thrones and exalts the humble. This is the God of Joseph who turns for good everything that the enemy intends for harm. Still resounding in my spirit are those silent words of my heart that rose up against the enemy in the midst of persecution:

As for you, you meant evil against me, but God meant it for good in order to bring about this present result, to preserve many people alive (Genesis 50:20).

Not only did God set into motion these extraordinary reversals and transfers of space and resource, but He saw to it that later, during the ISIS years, the highest British military commander became my worship leader in the embassy chapel. This for me was a great prophetic symbol of Judah (praise) occupying the frontline in the battle and of the establishment of the throne through praise and worship. Having the highest British military commander, General Roddy Porter, lead worship somehow completed our great story. Even now his life is dedicated to worship and ministry and I have the honor of being the Patron of Military Ministries International of which he is the CEO. Worship is about taking ground; it is military—where the people worship, the kingdom is established because God is enthroned upon the praises of His people. Where there is worship, the throne is established.

So it was that we were seeing the laws and the principles of the kingdom being played out before our eyes. For me and my people, the days of pain were also days of awe. As violence and political tension were increasing, so were revelation and enlightenment. I learned the new covenant reality that there is a certain place (even within terror) where each day can be day of awe. It is the reality of constantly being aware of the presence of the Almighty.

For a short while after the end of the war when it was too dangerous for me to enter the red zone and hold church services at the St. George's Church building, God intervened and provided me with a Christian, God-fearing US Marine security commander who happened to have the highest security clearance within the military and diplomatic community. He had a unique authority to allow people to cross into the protected green zone. This man, who remains a close friend and colleague, single-handedly managed to bring several hundreds of people from the red zone into the green zone where we would meet for worship in the prime minister's office. This was a further example of divine reversal as the center of governance and executive decision-making became a place of divine activity. The place of secular political ministry became the place of a superior ministry—and this was all with the Shia prime minister's authorization.

One of many horrific moments was coming face to face with Saddam Hussein's former torture room. In 2004, not long after the end of the 2003 war, I was taken by my good friend, Mr. Yonadam Kanna, the Christian leader of the newly formed Assyrian Democratic Party to a room that was painted in dark blood red. Horrific crimes had been perpetrated here and in the center of the room were gutters and pipes. These gutters had been designed to channel human blood out of the building. Worse still, my eyes saw the imprints of smashed human bodies across certain walls. Anyone who opposed the regime had been barbarically killed.

It was with a sense of consolation that Mr. Kanna explained to me how this torture chamber had now been converted into the office of the Commission of Human Rights. The place of violation under the old regime was now destined to become a place for the promotion of justice, reconciliation—a safe place where people could recount their stories and have their voices heard.

In the early stages of acquiring the building, the authorities did not transform the space instantly, as they wanted the crimes of the past to be exposed. Now, however, there is a whole new space and an ambience of justice and calmness. Once again, this is a radical story of divine reversal and a picture of God's ability and desire to reclaim territory and turn everything around. Other smaller torture rooms were converted into residential and teaching rooms such as those in the Iraqi Institute of Peace of which I was President. The soundtrack of enmity, hatred and death had been replaced with a soundtrack of meaningful biblically based education on conflict resolution and reconciliation. A new zone was being created.

During my time in Baghdad, I returned for short periods to Jerusalem where I would meet my wife and sons on school breaks and visit friends in the orthodox Jewish community and Messianic community. These breaks were always a time when I would have fresh encounters with God particularly at the Garden Tomb or at the Western Wall. The Jaffa gate area of the Old City has always been (and still is) for me a place of divine connections and reconnections with people from different nations. Many of my moments there have been deeply prophetic in nature and filled with a tangible sense of the glory.

One day in 2012 at the time of the ISIS uprisings, I returned to Jerusalem for a break after experiencing a violent onslaught from Iraqi terrorists against our Christian community. All of their Bibles had been destroyed and burned, the sense of theft and violation was unbearable, and feeling deeply distressed on behalf on my people I took a flight to Jerusalem in order to clear my mind and spend focused time in prayer.

I was praying in the courtyard of Christ Church that God would release a divine solution to this crisis of sacrilege and destruction and grant holy recompense to our people who had been robbed of their most precious item, when suddenly I was approached by a gentleman whom I had never met before.

The gentleman was from Northern Ireland and his name was Mr. Brad Turkington. He knew about my work from the media, and after he introduced himself his first question was, "Tell me, Andrew, how are you doing for Bibles?" Well as the crisis was so prominent in my mind, I expressed to him my torment and informed him that my peoples' Bibles had been stolen and destroyed by terrorists. It was hard to retain the tears as I explained that their Bibles were in heaps of ashes lying amidst the ruins of buildings and the decomposing corpses of innocent Christians who had not yet been recovered from beneath the rubble.

As I poured out my heart, I had no idea who Mr. Turkington was and assumed he was just a regular visitor or tourist voicing concern for the people of Baghdad. However, I soon realized that this was a divinely orchestrated encounter and that through this man God was about to present Himself as our "very present help in time of need." Having listened to my response, Mr. Turkington reached into his bag and took out of it a small device that looked similar to a mobile phone. He said, "Andrew, I have these solar-powered audio Bibles; would you be interested in having them for your people in Baghdad? We have them in both Arabic and English."

As you could imagine, on seeing these small solar-powered devices I became even more emotional and wept tears of pain and joy. I was overwhelmed with how incredibly faithful our Father is. He had planned and foreseen that my time of prayer be intercepted by the man who held the answer to the prayer.

The Holy Ghost has the latest news from the God-head and has designed for us the right place and the right time. Events happen in a remarkable way. You drop in right where the need is.[1]

For me, it was about the thief versus the Father. The enemy is a thief, a criminal, a terrorist, and a crook. He has created nothing, and he stands in war against the Father. The enemy has no legal rights to property or territory other than those that mankind gives to him, and he specializes in anarchy, hijack, shipwreck, kidnapping, captivity, sabotage, and theft. The Father, however, is the redeemer, the restorer, and the giver of life: *"The thief comes only to steal and kill and destroy; I came that they may have life, and have it abundantly"* (John 10:10).

The Father is never late; He is just on time. I felt the weight of His presence overshadow me and comfort my soul. In heartache I had prayed, worshiped, and reached into the glory which was now releasing into my hand the solutions and reversals of Heaven. The glory realm is the realm of divine solutions. That which the enemy had robbed was being quickly restored.

Within a few weeks every single person in our church in Iraq had a solar-powered audio Bible. We had little electricity and power, but ample sun, which was all we required. The joyful gratitude among our people was immense. I particularly remember the gratitude and delight among the several blind people in our church who suddenly for the first time could regularly hear the Bible.

In a recent email conversation with Tom Treseder, the president of MegaVoice, the company that supplies the solar-powered Bibles, he described the process of invention and the way in which

God enabled him in the 1980s to create a durable device that would withstand the harsh conditions of mission fields. Mr. Treseder is a man of great faith and divine favor who received the blueprints from Heaven to collaborate with specialists based in Galilee. The result was a silicone-based device that continues to equip millions all over the globe:

> I asked the Lord to enable me to create a Bible with no moving parts, easy to use by the world's blind, and that was water, sand and vermin-proof, robust and powered by the sun, where the message would be secure and could not be indiscriminately tampered with or destroyed. Some people scoffed at such a crazy dream. Such a thing did not exist in 1987, it seemed impossible. But spurred on by the words of the Lord Jesus, "With man it is impossible, but with God all things are possible," and with a band of other inspired and gifted colleagues, centered on the shores of Galilee, God enabled in 1988, my earlier prayer to be answered.

My response to this is simply, "What a gift to humanity! What a good and faithful Father!" He is the inventor of all inventors, His mind is magnificently impenetrable, He is the God of the macro and the micro. Let us never forget how intelligent, meticulous, and all-seeing He is; He does not just reverse but He restores, and when He restores it is always superior to the original. He did not just redeem the Bibles to the people of Iraq, but He supplied durable, concealable devices and He supplied for the blind.

As I write, I am also reminded of an occasion prior to this when a truck of illustrated Iraqi children's Bibles destined for the children of our community was diverted en route to Iraq by the Mahdi army—a highly violent, Shiite organization known for robbing and pillaging vehicles that transported aid from the West. The Bibles were stolen, and our Iraqi children had no resource. A few months later a man called Ali entered one of our offices and approached me. He was one of the senior members of the Mahdi army and a dangerous man of ill repute. He addressed me as "Abouna" (father), spoke to me about the children, and left the room. Five minutes later he returned to the office with stacks of illustrated children's Bibles—the very ones that had been stolen. God had sovereignly intervened and caused the thief to return that which had been stolen.

Reflections

In all of our lives there are situations, patterns, cycles, symbols, statements that may seem irreversible. Yet one of the most powerful realities that I experienced during my time in Iraq was that of radical divine reversal. This reality lies at the very heart of God's restorative and redemptive nature. No man can reverse the sovereign actions of God, only God can reverse the actions of man. We see this in the book of Esther:

> *If it please the king, and if I have favour in his sight, and the thing seem right before the king, and I be pleasing in his eyes, let it be written to **reverse** the letters devised by Haman the son of Hammedatha the Agagite, which he wrote to destroy the Jews*

which are in all the king's provinces (Esther 8:5-6 KJV).

Esther sought the King's favor to enforce a sovereign reversal of the letters of evil intent written by Haman. She saw to it that the death sentence awaiting her people was not simply withdrawn but fully reversed and replaced by a display of favor, honor, and divine recompense that included the immediate removal of the oppressor.

> *Seal it with the king's ring: for the writing which is written in the king's name, and sealed with the king's ring, may no man* **reverse** (Esther 8:8 KJV).

Esther was equally aware of the king's authority and legitimacy and she knew that the placement of the royal seal was a sovereign act that no man could reverse. This is a wonderful picture of the outstretched arm of the Lord interrupting, overriding, and radically reversing the schemes of the enemy.

Reversal and regression originally took place when Adam and Eve turned from God's original perfect plan. When we repent and return to Him, we give Him permission to reset the direction and to override the reversal of the enemy by reversing the curse and restoring all that has been subverted. Jesus reversed the curse once and for all when He rose from the grave, and it is our inheritance to know the reality of this reversal in our daily lives.

Prayer

Father, as the psalmist proclaims, You are the one who "changes the wilderness into a pool of water and a dry land into springs of water" (Ps. 107:35). I declare this reality over every wilderness represented by the readers of this book. I thank You that You are an intentional God, the God who intervenes and brings the realm of Heaven to earth. You overturn negative reports; You override medical diagnoses, and You reverse the curse. You are the God of radical, dramatic reversals, and I ask that those reading be amazed by Your activity in and around them in the days ahead.

Note

1. Wigglesworth, *The Anointing of His Spirit*, 58.

CHAPTER FIVE

SOVEREIGN PROVIDER

I TALKED IN THE LAST CHAPTER OF THE GREAT REVERSALS of ground, space, and resource and the transfers that God initiates for the benefit of His people and for the establishment of His domain—the kingdom being the King's domain. In the same way we saw God show Himself in our midst as the faithful provider, the God of more than enough. We learned to become reliant on His magnitude, His superior ability, and His wealth. The miracles we saw inspired awe not simply because of their existence but because of the deep eternal lessons hidden in each one.

A significant degree of my work involves traveling across the world in order to lecture at different universities and speak in churches, conferences, and political settings. Shortly after the war I was speaking at Griggs Green Christian School in Seattle. I had been invited to speak to the students there because the deputy head mistress was married to one of my senior military men (a Tops Officer in the Secret Services). I gave an assembly to around two hundred children between the ages of six and fourteen. This was by no means a fundraising event; I was talking to the children about the goodness of God and telling them a little about my life in Baghdad, how God turned up in extraordinary ways, and how He would do the same for them. At the end of the assembly as the students were returning to lessons, a nine-year-old boy named Sean approached my chair and silently handed me one single dollar. I thanked him sincerely for his kindness, and he smiled and walked away in silence. I was touched by this young boy's act of courage in approaching me and wondered what had moved him to do it. I kept the dollar note in my Bible so I would never forget this simple yet deeply moving act of kindness.

I then journeyed from Seattle to Redding, California where I was speaking to the students at the Bethel School of Supernatural Ministry. At one point when I was teaching on the law of sowing and reaping and the importance of simple childlike giving, I happened to refer to the young boy at Griggs Green School in Seattle who, on the previous day, had given me a one-dollar note. As I recounted the short story, suddenly a whole stream of students arose from their seats and came to the front with one-dollar bills throwing them down on the stage until there was a huge heap of money sitting right there in front of me. Row after row of students came until the entire lecture theatre was full of students emptying their pockets. I had no idea that my reference to one kind, courageous nine-year-old would turn into a tidal wave of dollars. Sean's small, singular seed of faith and sacrifice led to an epic harvest. His act reminded me of the young boy with fish and loaves, when one boy's sacrifice established the momentum for a wave of exponential increase and radical multiplication.

As I continued to tell the one-dollar story around the world, the figure dramatically increased, and I can tell you with confidence that Sean's one-dollar bill, which grew to $25,000 on that particular trip, led to a grand total of over $4.7 million cash being raised for Iraqi Christians within one year. This money enabled us to completely restore and open a clinic and school within the church grounds in Baghdad. It also enabled us to intensify our relief project within the community and give generously to the Mother Teresa home we were helping to finance during this period. The outcome was overwhelming, and as I travel I continue to keep a one-dollar note in my Bible as a reminder of God's provision.

What did I learn from this experience? First, I was reminded that many of our greatest ambassadors, pioneers, inspirers, influencers, and groundbreakers are children. I have always known and experienced this. Second, one simple act of courage and obedience can cause the floodgates to open and create a shift that releases the intentions of God. Third, every individual's "little" can collectively change a region, potentially a nation, and by the same principle, a continent, a hemisphere, the entire world. Fourth, through this simple process I saw the profound reality of a "wounded part of Christ's body" being ministered to by the rest of the body—the global church united in releasing God's goodness. For most people who gave, the giving of one dollar was not "sacrificial giving" (of course, for some it was), but this was an act of *united giving*. When a human body is wounded, each microscopic white blood cell works to bring healing. This image is not one of great faith and sacrifice; it is one of each cell functioning according to its purpose and created design. Should it not be the same with us? Of course, there is a place and a moment for radical, sacrificial giving, but does not the primary reality of giving and sharing relate to each of us functioning unitedly in our call to heal the parts of our humanity that our wounded? These are the thoughts that have moved upon my heart.

Divine Provision of Lego

Another great act of divine orchestration leading to timely provision related to the Danish ambassador, Ambassador Bo Weber. The Danish embassy was in the secure green zone next door to the military compound where I lived. The Christmas period was drawing near, resources were low, and I was discussing with colleagues how on earth we were going to provide gifts for our children. "Well, Father Andrew, you do know that my nation is home to one of the largest toy companies in the world?" said the Danish ambassador. "Leave it with me. I will contact Lego and see what we can do."

"That would be great," I replied, thinking how exciting it would be for each family to have a little box of Lego to open and share on Christmas day.

A few weeks later, a Charlie 130 landed and it was raining Legos, so many Legos, more Legos, and more. The military had collected it from a Danish plane landing in Kuwait and brought it back to Baghdad. We had an overflow of brand-new Legos, the equivalent of a factory full packed from floor to ceiling, and we soon became the only church in the Middle East to have its own official "Lego Room." We had such an abundance of Legos, we gave boxes of it to all the communities of every faith and to various public places across the region. As the Christmas season drew near, Iraq turned into Legoland.

As you can imagine, our children's play experience was transformed. We had young builders, creators, inventors, designers, architects in our midst, and I was reminded once again of the limitlessness of divine providence. Jesus tells us: *"seek first His kingdom and His righteousness, and all these things will be added to you"* (Matt. 6:33). Whether for children or adults, He is the God of "all these things." He is the provider of the small and the big; He is the God of "all these things."

The Lego room become a microcosm of the expanded congregation and of the rebuilding that was going on around us. Order, alignment, and color were being restored. I still remain inspired by the Lego company motto: "Only the best is good enough." This speaks to me of the way in which God treats His children well. There is nothing mediocre about Him; He is extravagant in all His ways. I was equally interested to learn that Ole Kirk Kristiansen, the inventor and founder of Lego, was himself a man born into extreme poverty, a man of strong faith with a heart to help others by building and improving church buildings, supporting missions, and training young boys in the carpentry trade. Mr. Kristiansen was also a man who had known tragedy, having lost his wife at a young age and being left as a widower with four children to raise. Knowing something of its inventor's life made our Lego room all the more significant. I still have a sense of this man rejoicing in Heaven on our behalf.

The Danes continued to provide for us very significantly during the time of turmoil, and we created a memorial within St. George's church for the Danish soldiers killed in Baghdad.

Furthermore, my work and ministry have other significant links to Denmark, a link that I would have never predicted before moving to Iraq. Though the Iraqi children could obviously not speak Danish, they all sang the Danish national anthem perfectly whenever the Danish ambassador came to visit us.

The current patron of my organization who resides in Jerusalem is of Danish origin. He is the current chief rabbi of Norway and from a long line of chief rabbis in Denmark. His name is Chief Rabbi Michael Melchior and, as well as becoming one of my closest friends from since his time in the Israeli government, he has been instrumental in our work of reconciliation and a great voice of peace and fraternity. Rabbi Melchior was very involved with me during the Bethlehem siege and in the establishment of the Alexandrian agreement—a great historic declaration of peace between Christian, Jewish, and Muslim leaders. Interestingly, Copenhagen became the place for key international reconciliation meetings in 2005, meetings that were facilitated by the great hospitality and generosity of the Danes, who under a new ambassador once again showed a unique desire to pay, protect, provide, and be a practical solution in times of crisis. Many of these meetings were held in the Bishop of Copenhagen's palace. The various Danish bishops I met were really marked by a sense of unusual compassion.

Several years later when ISIS moved in to Baghdad and launched a major onslaught against the Christians, the two nations to first reach out to us were Israel and Denmark. When ISIS started to emerge in 2010, it was Israel who came to our rescue. Israel had the greatest intelligence under Benyamin Netanyahu and Shimon Perez. I regularly met with the Israeli Ministry of Foreign Affairs in Jerusalem and even though they could not practically come and assist, they sent a very key NGO called Israel Aid who provided on-the-ground medical and financial help to the people in Kurdistan while providing those of us in Baghdad with key intelligence and defense information. The Israelis wanted to come to Baghdad, and we discussed the possibility, but it was simply too dangerous for them or us. Nevertheless, they were a highly supportive presence in times of need and I often felt that they were an older brother reaching out their hand to us.

Meanwhile, it was Denmark who once again came to our rescue by fully financing a key meeting of Iraqi religious leaders in order to proclaim an Islamic (*fatwa*) injunction against the persecution of Christians. Though most foreign ambassadors expected this to fail, my people gathered to pray for the outcome of the meeting, and we met with success—from the hour of the injunction, the persecution stopped for almost a year and thousands of lives were preserved.

Why Denmark? I believe there are hidden reasons and connections that God has yet to reveal to me; however, one aspect that God has revealed to me regarding the significance of Denmark in blessing and enabling my work lies in their singularity of identity as the only European nation who ardently and actively sought to save and protect its Jews during the Holocaust—a period very central to my own academic and theological journey.

Throughout the years of its power, the Danish government consistently refused to accept German demands regarding unequal treatment of Jews and the Danish monarch, King Christian X, was clear regarding the protective role of the Danish constitution. The Danish authorities refused to align with anti-Jewish legislation in the shocking way that other nations did, and unlike those Jews so unfortunate to be residing in France, Danish Jews were not forced to wear yellow stars. Their civil rights were fully protected and remained equal to those of the rest of the population. Over a two-month evacuation period, the vast majority of Danish Jews were transported to a place of safety in neutral Sweden by means of fishing boats and motorboats.

Though many Danish Jews lost their lives in Theresienstadt, the role of the Danish people in forming a resistance was remarkable. The resistance consisted of Danes from all walks of life—intellectuals, priests, policemen, medics, factory workers—and many regular people contributed by running errands and sending food parcels and provisions to their Jewish countrymen. This united public response was intensified by constant requests from the Danish Red Cross for visits to be made to those who had been deported to Theresienstadt. Meanwhile a Danish wartime politician named John Christmas Møller, who had fled to England in 1942, became a popular commentator due to his broadcasts to the nation over the BBC. He also played an important role in London as a broadcaster for BBC Radio's Danish language service aimed at occupied Denmark. He spoke strongly against any form of collaboration with Germany and promoted active resistance.

When I thus consider the significant contribution of the Danes to those who have suffered, I contemplate the role of Denmark historically as a host, a provider, and a protector. The Danes have been a distinct voice of fraternity, equality, love, hope, and social justice in many times of crisis. When I picture the overflowing Lego room, I remember God's power and His providence and I reflect on His tender care for the children. For me, the Lego says it all: Lean Entirely on God's Omnipotence.

Toys for Tots

Another great act of Christmas provision took place when we realized once again that with an ever-growing congregation and an ever-increasing community, we could not afford to buy gifts for the children. I remember us gathering to pray for increased financial provision during one of our embassy meetings, and after our time of prayer I was approached by a US Marine. He spoke to me about a US Marines initiative called "Toys for Tots." He explained to me about how "Toys for Tots" had been founded as a Los Angeles charity in 1947 by Major Bill Hendricks. The foundation had been inspired by his wife Diane who, when wanting to donate a homemade ragdoll to a needy child, was unable to find an organization to assist her. At her suggestion, Major Hendricks gathered a group of local Marine reservists who coordinated and collected several thousand toys for local children that year from collection stations that they had set up outside Warner Bros. cinemas. Their efforts were so successful that, in 1948, "Toys for Tots' was launched as a national campaign.

My new friend from the Marines explained to me that they wanted to expand into Iraq and that now was their chance. This would be the first time since its creation in 1947 that the charity would be able to provide for the children of Iraq. It was an exciting moment for me, and I knew the Marine had been sent to us "for such a time as this." Many other coalition soldiers and non-military people from embassies all over the world donated to us and once again our children were given gifts for Christmas and experienced the extravagant blessings of a God who cared for their every need. The reality of Second Corinthians 9:8—the limitless of God's goodness and His desire to respond to "all things at all times"—became part of our reality.

> *And God is able to bless you abundantly, so that **in all things at all times**, having all that you need, you will abound in every good work* (NIV).

"Want Some Meat?"

I will now tell you about another memorable occasion of sudden divine provision that relates to one of my weekly visits to the home of the Grand Ayatollah Khadamia. The grand Ayatollah was one of three very senior Shiite leaders in Iraq. These men are involved in religious and political decision-making, and I had a very positive relationship with them. They were good men who had their own secret police and whose goal was to protect the people from Saddam Hussein and provide for the nation to the best of their ability.

I visited Grand Ayatollah Khadamia weekly (he was one of those who had come with me to meet Billy Graham when he assisted me in convening a huge gathering of religious leaders in the US). Ayatollah Khadamia would cook lavishly and roast a whole sheep for his guests, and as a strict vegetarian at the time I stayed with fish and vegetables while my security guards and associates enjoyed the sheep. One day just after the 2003 invasion of Iraq, I was sitting in the Ayatollah's saloon and he said to me, "Abouna Andrew, we are in a desperate situation; the nation of Iraq is running out of food. Very soon we will have nothing."

I replied, "Ayatollah, I have only twelve dollars in my pocket and our foundation would never be in a position to finance the amount that you require."

His response was full of urgency and passion: "But Abouna, you can pray, you must pray, and God will provide."

So it was that early that evening I prayed fervently for divine provision and for God to show His glory to the nation. I was praying on my balcony, which looked over the edge of the Tigris river, when suddenly I saw a ball of fiery orange red and white hovering over the length of the river. This was not the sun setting, nor was it any recognizable occurrence. It was an enormous ball of glowing, blazing, fiery light that was not very high up, just a few feet above the river and it stretched the length of the river. I was absolutely perplexed and overwhelmed; never in my life had I seen anything remotely like it. "Father," I said, "what on earth is this?" I then heard God tell me to read Ezekiel. Of course, I had read it several times but not recently and not with the fresh lens that my eyes had just received. I had forgotten how long Ezekiel was, but I read the whole book, prayed again, and went to bed.

The following morning while I was sitting at breakfast, a Jewish man called Andy, who was part of the US military personnel, a man whom I had never met before, walked over to me and pulled a chair up to the table so that he could sit down next to me. "Hey, Father!" he said in a rather loud, stern voice. "My name is Andy, do you want some meat?"

"What do you mean?" I asked.

He repeated his statement and I repeated my reply. Finally, he asked a third time and when I asked how much meat he was referring to. He replied, "Oh, just a few thousand tons."

Well, there and then—the day after the Ayatollah had exhorted me to pray to *my* God—the nation of Iraq found itself with enough meat to feed every village of every town of every region—a good choice of halal beef, chicken, and lamb. The explanation that came later was that one of the large Charlie 130 planes, carrying meat for the coalition military, had undergone confusion with its paperwork meaning that the meat was now spare. The meat was taken from the plane and put on military lorries with fridges in them. From there it was taken to all of the big Shia bases called *hawza* and distributed to the people. I may have been a herbivore at the time, but by divine orchestration, which is always perfect and always on time, I was able to see to it that the nation ate good meat.

Reflections

As I pondered on the glory cloud, I sensed in my spirit that it had been a sign of the power of God being "present to provide" in the same way that we talk of His power being "present to heal." Divine glory and divine provision are deeply connected. Where Heaven is manifest, His wealth is manifest, His overflow is manifest. His providence is a result and an outflow of His glory. *"And my God will supply all your needs according to His riches in glory in Christ Jesus"* (Phil. 4:19).

God's provision often came in other ways through the provision of caliber people, key leaders, and national governments that stood alongside us politically and militarily, such as Great Britain, America, Denmark, and South Korea. General Mick Kicklighter, the representative of the Office of White House Liaison in Baghdad, was a great spiritual friend and mentor. After the war he became the overseer of the Pentagon generally. Likewise, former National Security Advisor Bud McFarlane was a powerful prayer warrior and a great strength to our ministry. President G.W. Bush was also highly supportive of our work and these, among several other Christian politicians, military personnel, and leaders within the coalition provided me with insight, encouragement, and friendship, enabling me to see that when earthly power and divine glory come together, there are limitless possibilities to seeing the favor of God released.

Prayer

Consider the ravens, for they neither sow nor reap; they have no storeroom nor barn, and yet God feeds them; how much more valuable you are than the birds! (Luke 12:24)

Father, I ask for fresh revelation to be imparted to each person reading this regarding their identity as Your treasured possession. They are highly valued in Your sight and it is Your will to reveal Yourself as sovereign provider in every area of their lives. I ask that You release faith and patience to wait for Your superior solutions and and that each reader experiences Your outstretched arm reaching perfectly into their situation. Reward all those who have been faithful sowers with an abundant harvest that bears Your signature.

CHAPTER SIX

EXPERIENCING TANGIBLE GLORY

TWO DAYS FOLLOWING THE MIRACULOUS PROVISION OF resources described in the previous chapter, I entered deeper and further into what I can only describe as a realm of glorious divine presence. It seemed that one door opened to another and that God was allowing me to journey into glimpses of His majesty.

It was a hot, sunny day and I was on a journey in search of Ezekiel's tomb. This is a sacred place for the Jewish people, and my friends from Israel called me to say there were rumors it had been destroyed by terrorists. I had heard that the site was within traveling distance and even though I do not particularly enjoy visiting tombs, shrines, and religious sites, I was eager to locate the place of the prophet's burial and to be able to update my Jewish friends. After a long, arduous journey, which involved being trapped in a "donkey jam" for several hours, we eventually arrived. People in the region traveled on donkeys on tracks, and the actual location of the tomb was very near Babylon in southern Iraq. The tomb was housed inside an ancient Jewish synagogue in a Shia-controlled area between Babylon and Najaf.

Before entering the synagogue, I saw several clouds of bright, radiant light similar to those I had seen over the Tigris. These clouds were about thirty feet above us and they were full of light. We gazed at what I can only describe as a mesmerizing spectacle of spinning wheels. (This was not a vision but a drama—visible to the physical eyes.) There were about five wheels; they were not colored, just white—full of radiant, white light and spinning round and round. I was with General Georges Sada (a former senior Air Vice Marshall who became my Chief of Staff), and we stood in awe and watched the spinning wheels for about five minutes before entering the synagogue. General Sada witnessed everything I did, and we were overwhelmed to the point of being speechless.

We then entered the synagogue, which sadly was now functioning as a Shia mosque despite looking clearly like a synagogue. We stood beneath the *bimah*, the canopy beneath which the Torah was read, and could feel a tangible presence. It was during these moments at Ezekiel's tomb that, despite my not having anticipated it, I had the strongest physical sensation of the weight of God's glory that I have ever felt in my whole ministry. We then entered a side room where the shrine was held—the Shiites respected Ezekiel as a prophet so they had taken good care of the shrine allowing a constant stream of Shia visitors to visit daily. Most of Ezekiel chapter 43 was engraved in ancient Hebrew into the cream marble ceiling and all of the verses spoke about the glory of the Lord in the

Temple. I went home and re-read Ezekiel 43, and as I did the sense of God's presence overwhelmed me once again.

This was an amazing experience for so many reasons. It had been such a challenge to even locate the site, and though I personally had never had much interest in visiting sacred sites, there was a significance to this place. Such was the depth and intensity of its impact on my spiritual life that I returned there every month. Each time, I had dramatic encounters and experiences; I did not see the spinning wheels again (though others described having similar visions), but I did see angelic beings with my physical eyes. They were enormous, radiant, white-garmented men exactly the same as the ones who appeared regularly in Baghdad and were seen by children and adults in the congregation.

After this experience I started to take adults and children from the church on trips to Ezekiel's tomb. Many of my people experienced the same tangible sense of God's presence and some had visions of what they described as "angelic creatures." Each visit was marked by a deep awareness of the majestic presence of God, which increased my sensitivity to the divine supernatural realm and my desire to experience more of God. These were the first times that I felt the real density of the glory—the *kabod*—the physical weight of His presence, though not a burdensome heaviness. In the depths of God's presence, there was a weight that outweighed every other weight of living in a war zone. This is the paradox of the glory. As I mentioned, the word *kabod* literally means "weight" and relates to the tangible presence of Jesus, yet this is the Jesus whose burden is *light*. The weight of His presence shifts every other oppressive weight and enables one to feel nothing but Him. I like the way that Ruth Ward Heflin, in her book *Revelation Glory*, describes this reality:

> The weight of glory that comes upon us is about as heavy as cotton candy. The heaviness of the Spirit is light. There is no other way to describe it.[1]

A further experience I had of the manifest presence of the glory relates to gold. As I mentioned in Chapter Three, I first experienced the supernatural manifestation of gold in Israel when mediating the negotiation of hostages during the Bethlehem siege and leading meetings on conflict resolution. My second experience was back in Jerusalem following the period of great turmoil surrounding the Bethlehem siege when Jumana (who had been one of my former interns) became critically ill. Jumana was a Coptic Christian from a very devout family. Just a few months into her study of English and education at the Hebrew University of Jerusalem, she was admitted into the emergency medical unit at the Hadassah Hospital, and after serious lung, kidney, and spleen surgery, she quickly developed septicemia and came very near to death.

As faith rose inside of me, I chose to discard my medical mind and believe that the medical report was not the final report. We reached into Heaven and believed God for a mighty miracle. For a period of forty days with Ruth Ward Heflin's assistant, Connie Wilson, and several of my friends and key leaders, we spent many hours interceding, fasting, and worshiping at Jumana's bedside. On several occasions during times of worship and intercession, we saw supernatural gold appear on Jumana and her whole body would be glittering. This manifestation became a sure sign to me that the wonder was to follow. I had seen the sign and I was anticipating the wonder. Though Jumana was not expected to live for long and was very close to death, I was convinced that we would see resurrection glory.

Literally on day forty-one, Jumana suddenly started to regain consciousness. The doctors were astonished, and though our faith was strong I must admit we were shocked by the suddenness of God's intervention. We had learned so much by unrelentingly contending for Jumana's life and it may have been long, hard forty days of death in the wilderness, but it was in the wilderness that we found gold.

My third experience of being covered in gold was in the early months of 2003 when attending a meeting at the Pentagon in the Office of White House Liaison in the Department of Defense. In this meeting an important decision was being made by the White House and the Department of Defense with regard to the removal of Saddam. There was no one in the US government who had any real experience of being in Iraq under the Saddam regime. They had no logical reason to commission me as "advisor" as I personally have no military experience; however, I did have immense experience of being in Iraq, and I was acutely aware of the oppression of the people under this regime. God orchestrated the entire meeting and confirmed His will to remove evil and release the oppressed by a sudden manifestation of gold dust that covered several key members of the meeting such as the Secretary of Defense, Donald Rumsfeld, other key ministers, including me. Though it was a secular military, many of those present were believers and the sudden mysterious manifestation of gold was recognized as a sign of God's presence. It was only later, when I began to see in more detail the unfolding of my own assignment and the reality of the glory within the war zone, that I began to reflect on the magnitude of this experience in the Pentagon.

My fourth experience of gold manifestations was in England around the year of 2003 at the Detling Bible Week, which was an annual summer Bible camp held at the Kent county showground in the south of England. It was a vibrant gathering of up to four thousand passionate Spirit-filled believers, desperate to experience the presence of God. The worship was always powerful and intense. I was one of the two speakers for the week, and one night when I got up to speak after a time of deep worship I could sense the presence of Jesus in our midst. As I looked at those gathered, I could see that seemingly every person was covered in gold. There were many photographs, reports, and blogs written by those who were at this Bible week. On this particular night the gold lasted for around two hours. There must have been few, if any, who were present in the tent and did not experience it. Also, during this week, I experienced manifestations of silver. These signs are God's way of attracting our attention and elevating our faith to reach into the unseen realm. They have been experienced by many people all over the world and are a visible sign of the glory and majesty of the Father, Son, and Spirit. Throughout the last few decades, there have been many documented and photographed experiences involving supernatural gold, silver, diamonds, other jewels, and aromatic oil as well as fully documented medical reports of instant miraculous healings, creative miracles, and financial miracles that have occurred in the atmosphere of the glory.

It seemed that the whole gathering was glittering in God's glory. There was an atmosphere of revival, and several people were lying on the floor in deep prayer for a long period of time. It was during this conference that I met one of a few key people who would be instrumental to the support of our Iraqi Christians and established several divinely orchestrated relationships with people. However, my most overwhelming memory is not the divine favor, nor the spectacular visible presence of God's glory, but the sense of awe and hunger to see and know more of the majestic splendor of King Jesus. The timing of the event was crucial to my assignment as it was just after this very deep encounter with God that I was called to take on permanent work in Iraq and rebuild the ruins of the church community in Baghdad.

Once again, it was only later as I experienced the unfolding of God's plan and gained a clearer vision of the blueprints He was releasing that I saw the real impact and significance of those deep, glorious encounters that preceded my move to Baghdad.

Reflections

Signs and wonders do not always come together. The sign—whether a prophetic word, a dream, a vision, a manifestation, an angelic visitation, or some other experience of the divine supernatural—often leads into a gradual, progressive unfolding of God's purpose that leads to the wonder. Often the unfolding of God's intentions is itself the wonder as one observes the great mysterious and majestic hand of God intervening in one's situation. I imagine it was rather like this for Mary—the sign that was the miraculous pregnancy, led to the wondrous unfolding of a wonder, as she beheld in her womb He who was both a sign and a wonder. Some would embrace His glory; others, in their blindness, would deny and oppose it.

*And Simeon blessed them and said to Mary His mother, "Behold, this Child is appointed for the fall and rise of many in Israel, and for a **sign** to be opposed"* (Luke 2:34).

Prayer

Father, I thank You for the gift of holy hunger, and I pray that all who long for it experience increased levels of Your manifest presence. Father, I ask for an enlargement of perspectives and a renewal of mindsets as we choose to fix our minds on things above and submit to Heaven's logic. I ask that as the reader feasts upon Your Word, leans into You, worships You, and rests in Your presence, they experience an outbreak of signs, wonders, and miracles and the sudden, visible activity of Heaven within their world. Overwhelm them, Jesus, with Your presence so that everything negative becomes exceedingly small.

Note

1.   Ruth Ward Heflin, *Revelation Glory* (Hagerstown, MD: McDougal Publishing, 2000), 229.

CHAPTER SEVEN

THE MAN IN WHITE

As I mentioned earlier, the glory realm is the realm of His presence; it is the fullness of Jesus. The glory is more than an atmosphere, more than a spiritual sensation, more than an encounter with divine realities; the glory is a person. I cannot study the great men and women of the Old Testament as well as the Messianic prophecies without concluding that those who experienced the glory of God had glimpses of Jesus even if they did not know it. We are told by Jesus that even Abraham rejoiced to see His day.

As the prophet Joel foretold, visions of Jesus are becoming increasingly widespread and the transformations that follow these visions are always dramatic, leading to total consecration. Countless people all over the world are having visions of Jesus clothed in radiant white garments of light with a face that emanates pure light. Daniel and John both experienced the glory of His appearance.

As I looked, thrones were set in place, and the Ancient of Days took his seat. His clothing was as white as snow; the hair of his head was white like wool (Daniel 7:9 NIV).

In the middle of the lampstands I saw one like a son of man, clothed in a robe reaching to the feet, and girded across His chest with a golden sash. His head and His hair were white like white wool, like snow; and His eyes were like a flame of fire (Revelation 1:13-14).

During the years leading a church in Baghdad, I personally saw a total of fifty-eight Muslims place their faith in the deity of Jesus, convert to Christianity, and renounce their association with Islam. I have no doubt that there are countless other testimonies, but during two decades of ministry there I saw fifty-eight genuine conversions, ten of which were the radical conversions of extremely dangerous terrorists. What is interesting is that not once did I preach to a Muslim person or attempt to evangelize or convert them in any way. I simply ensured that they were made to feel valued and loved within our community, included in our relief programs, and welcome in our clinic. Conversion was dangerous and not a primary intent of my heart. My intent was to demonstrate love.

Religious identity, fervor, devotion, and allegiance in the Middle East are so strong that it takes more than persuasive words and free Bible courses to incite the Muslim people to suddenly switch allegiance and start worshiping another God. My prayer instead was that they would *see* Him. I asked Him to appear to them in their dreams as He has done to so many thousands, possibly millions, around the globe. From Iran to Japan and in so many other nations, there are recorded and unrecorded testimonies of people encountering Jesus in the night hours. At times, whole villages have converted after at least one person from each household recounted simultaneous dreams, visions, and visitations of Jesus in the night. The testimonies are all highly consistent and the conversions are documented with many claiming that Jesus presented to them His "holy book" and told them to acquire it and read it.

Regarding the conversions that I witnessed in Baghdad, each act of repentance resulted from a dramatic encounter with "the Man in White." The reported descriptions include Jesus appearing to them in blazing white garments, Jesus telling them that they must follow Him, Jesus announcing Himself as the Messiah, Jesus clothed in white filling their homes with overwhelming peace, Jesus appearing to them with dazzling eyes of love and passion, and Jesus calling them by name and saying to them, "I am the way." In every case, the conversion was *radical, fundamental,* and *extreme,* all of the words that we apply to terrorists and which should be applied to regular, faith-filled believers.

I remember being asked why Jesus always appeared in white and why so many of the dreams and visions were identical. All I can say is that when we read the visions of Ezekiel, Daniel, and John, we have a clear picture of the majestic radiance of the ascended Jesus.

White represents purity and holiness—the totality of light. Jesus Himself is the great light of both earth and Heaven. He made it clear on earth that He was the Light of the World and John, in his heavenly vision, witnessed this radiant light.

Muslims view white as the color of purity and peace; they wear white to pray on their holy days, and I find it significant that Jesus always appears to them in "their" holy color—a color they can relate to. One of the most memorable conversions that I witnessed was that of a man who was one of the senior leaders of ISIS. He was a highly dangerous criminal and one would never imagine him being capable of turning to God in repentance and humility. Yet this dark-minded terrorist was asleep one night when the man in white appeared to him and told him that he was Jesus Christ of Nazareth and the only way to God. This was like a modern-day Damascus Road experience where the perpetrator was confronted not by a prophet or an angel, but by Jesus Himself speaking on behalf of His persecuted church. As the apostle Paul stated of his former life:

> *For you have heard of my former manner of life in Judaism, how I used to persecute the church of God beyond measure and tried to destroy it* (Galatians 1:13).

After encountering the man in white, this dangerous ISIS terrorist immediately repented and converted without doubts or reservation. If the resurrected Jesus could appear to one of the most notorious terrorists of the early church and arrest him in light, we should not be surprised when it happens in our day. Saul, a devoted terrorist of his day was enlightened and counseled directly by Jesus, the Light who declared, "I am Jesus whom you are persecuting." I believe we will see a dramatic increase in these spiritual encounters. In many places, where there is no way of turning the hearts of men, King Jesus the chief rabbi, pastor, prophet, apostle, preacher, and evangelist will invade the dreams and visions of men, women, and children all over the world and apprehend them with the glorious bright white light of His presence.

One of the most memorable dreams experienced by two of the young people in my congregation were of Jesus in His radiant splendor. The dreams were powerful, timely gifts from Heaven, messages of consolation from a loving Father. It was around the year of 2014, and several families who had fled Baghdad and returned to Nineveh due to the violence in the capital were now being attacked by ISIS in the northern cities as this was also an area that was largely populated with Christians. We received news that amidst the explosions, kidnappings, burnings, and killings, four young children who were formerly a part of the St. George's congregation in Baghdad had been beheaded. The children were all between the ages of three and twelve, two boys and two girls. Eye witnesses, who had been there at the time of the attack, recounted the event: ISIS turned up at the family home a few days before the killings demanding that the father renounce his allegiance to Jesus Christ and pledge allegiance to Mohammed. They said that if he followed their command to turn to ISIS, his life would be spared. However, the father refused to convert and just a few days later they identified his children, captured them, and asked them the same question. The children refused to convert, openly declaring: "We love Jesus and we will always worship Him," and then they joined hands and started singing, "Jesus loves me this I know for the Bible tells me so." Following this the children were immediately shot by the terrorists and beheaded.

As you can imagine when the news reached me and the rest of my people in Baghdad (several hundred of whom I had already lost), we were overcome with sorrow, torment, and disgust. I remember feeling absolutely helpless and crying out to God on my bed. I wept like a broken man in a way that I have never wept before.

It was the following morning that the message of consolation came. Two girls who were friends but unrelated (both were still with me in Baghdad and from families who were very involved within the life of the church) came to see me as they both had had the same dream. In the dream, they had each been able to see through a window into Heaven where they saw Jesus dressed in garments of dazzling white dancing with the four children who had been beheaded and now had new bodies. They each described their dream to me in detail and they said, "Abouna Andrew, you must not cry anymore, for we have both seen our friends dancing in Heaven with Jesus." These dreamers were children who grew up seeing angels and experiencing miracles. The divine supernatural realm including the realm of dreams and visions was as real to them as their normal daily reality, so when they had these dreams they had full confidence that this was God speaking. As we know from scripture, God often confirms His word in the mouth of two witnesses, and so it was that my spirit was lifted and this vision became a source of joy. Often in places where fallen humanity appears to be at its most degraded, our revelation of divinity is at its most exalted. As Smith Wigglesworth states:

> The very place that was not fit for humanity was the
> place where John was most filled with God, and where
> he was most ready for the revelation of Jesus.[1]

On another occasion, a group of youth from my congregation were traveling on a bus through the highly dangerous red zone to get to the Friday night youth service. The bus exploded en route due to an IED (Intrinsic Explosive Device). This bus was not simply "surrounded" by explosions; the bus itself exploded and fell to pieces, yet miraculously not one of the children was injured. Though we were deeply relieved and thankful for the preserving hand of God, I was worried that the effects of the trauma would mean canceling a major event scheduled for Sunday. On that Sunday we had scheduled a special baptism for ten of the children and a time of anointing and blessing as they publicly affirmed their faith. This was an annual event that involved a huge amount of preparation and was followed by a special celebration. I thought we may have to postpone it as all ten of the young people being baptized had been on the bus and would feel shaken and emotionally fragile. However, when I suggested postponing the event, they were all genuinely shocked and assured me that they were absolutely fine and still excited about Sunday's event. One of the young boys smiled and shouted over to me: "Do not be worried for us, Abouna. Jesus was there with us in the bus. I had a vision of Him at the back of the bus, and He was dressed in white."

All of these examples are part of the reality of experiencing the glory zone within the war zone. Whether we perceive it or not, we must always be aware of God's nearness in times of trouble.

When I meditate on these encounters that people are having with the Man in White, especially people of other faiths, my heart is always drawn to the great call for all humanity to return to the image in which they were originally created. There is a call for humanity to "re-paint" itself, to allow itself to be redesigned and refashioned into the image of the divine Creator. That is to say, there is call and a promise for us also to be "garmented in white."

It is God's will that none should be lost, and His arms are open wide to those who will lay aside their pride and ignorance in order to "walk with Him in white."

> *But you have a few people in Sardis who have not soiled their garments; and they will walk with Me in white, for they are worthy. He who overcomes will thus be clothed in white garments; and I will not erase his name from the book of life, and I will confess his name before My Father and before His angels. He who has an ear, let him hear what the Spirit says to the churches* (Revelation 3:4-6).

It is the heart of God toward all of humanity to forsake their nakedness and find the true reason for which they were created. It is His will for every person to find the enrichment, the beauty, the dignity, and the clarity of vision that He alone has the sovereign power and will to endow.

> *I advise you to buy from Me gold refined by fire so that you may become rich, and white garments so that you may clothe yourself, and that the shame of your nakedness will not be revealed; and eye salve to anoint your eyes so that you may see* (Revelation 3:18).

The reality of Heaven is a reality that we can experience and walk in right here on earth. The call of the bride is to be radiant white just as the Lamb. To be garmented in His light is a high call; it means to abide within His glory, to be throne-focused, and to turn one's deepest affection and adoration toward no inferior pleasure.

Around the throne were twenty-four thrones; and upon the thrones I saw twenty-four elders sitting, clothed in white garments, and golden crowns on their heads (Revelation 4:4).

Reflections

The Greek word for *white* used in these verses is *leukai*—a word that does not simply refer to white as a color description but literally means "brilliant, bright, light" or "dazzling white." It is a word that denotes not simply the absence of darkness but the presence of a radiant person.

I love this statement by Gilbert Chesterton.

> [White] is not a mere absence of colour; it is a shining and affirmative thing, as fierce as red, as definite as black. ...God paints in many colours, but He never paints so gorgeously...as when He paints in white.[2]

Prayer

King of Glory, I thank You that we do not have to experience martyrdom and bloodshed to see You. Nor must we wait to pass from this world before we encounter You. Great King of Majesty, I ask that every person reading experience dreams, visitations, and encounters with You. I also pray that their friends, relatives, and loved ones who have not yet encountered You find themselves visited by You in person. Reveal Yourself to all of us, Jesus, as You did to Daniel, Ezekiel, and John.

Let us walk in the reality of Revelation 3:18, clothed in garments of white, enriched by Your supreme worth and value, and clear-sighted to see You as You are.

Notes

1. Wigglesworth, *The Anointing of His Spirit,* 152.
2. G.K. Chesterton, *In Defense of Sanity: The Best Essays of G.K. Chesterton,* "A Piece of Chalk," (San Francisco, CA: Ignatius Press, 2011).

Chapter Eight

Angels in Our Midst

I TALKED IN AN EARLIER CHAPTER OF MY EXPERIENCE OF the angelic realm in Bethlehem. These were my first experiences with angels and were a prelude to a more continuous and extensive awareness of and sensitivity to their protective role during the real war zone of Baghdad. As Joshua Mills so rightly states in his recent book *Moving in Glory Realms*:

> Where there is glory, there are angels, and where there are angels, there is glory. You can't separate them. These realms are intertwined with each other.[1]

The reality of the glory zone in the war zone was one in which angelic visitations and appearances were seemingly integrated organically into everyday life. At times, their presence amidst and around us was so visible, recognizable, and vivid there was a sense of them being an intrinsic part of our family and our landscape.

If I use the term "glory-scape" it may help me to explain how at certain times the angels were literally dotted around the church compound. We have photographs of them, some of which were published in one of my former books, *The Vicar of Baghdad*. Over ninety percent of angelic appearances that we witnessed were during or after times of deep worship. This should not be surprising as worship establishes the heavenly throne and declares His kingship. *"O You who are enthroned upon the praises of Israel. In You our fathers trusted; they trusted and You delivered them"* (Ps. 22:3-4).

Praise and worship release the realities of the kingdom of Heaven and attract the realm in which the throne is central—the realm of the glory. If deep, corporate worship establishes His throne and He is enthroned on the praises of His people, we should not be surprised when the realities and values of the throne room become part of our landscape.

> *And all the angels were standing around the throne and around the elders and the four living creatures; and they fell on their faces before the throne and worshiped God, saying, "Amen, blessing and glory and wisdom and thanksgiving and honor and power and might, be to our God forever and ever. Amen"* (Revelation 7:11-12).

Before I went to the Middle East, this would have been no more to me than an inspiring theory and an exciting reality to aspire to, but once I stepped into the darkness, solitude, and oppression experienced by Christian believers in Iraq, there was no space for theory. Theories are small; reality is limitless. Theories, methodologies, and principles can be helpful and encourage us to be trusting, adventurous, and experimental; however, the supernatural reality of Heaven crashing in is experiential, not experimental. We had no resources, no handbooks on angels, no schools of the supernatural, no schools of worship, no healing guide, no weekend retreats, no school of the prophets, yet we had the greatest training school that we could have ever prayed for—it was simply called "experiencing Jesus."

When the superficial façades beneath which we hide and the walls and barriers that we use to control the Holy Spirit and validate our lack of experience are removed, when all the boxes that we place God in are discarded and all of the props, luxuries, civil benefits, and worldly distractions are withdrawn, there is a space, a vacuum, a place that is big and empty enough to contain a larger and superior reality. We had a choice: we could fix our eyes on the bloodstained cityscape and attune our ears to the horrific sounds of missiles, or we could rise above it all and cultivate within our earthly chaos a space that was filled with Him.

The angels we experienced corporately generally appeared within the church compound; during these times we sensed an open Heaven and the tangible nearness of God. The angels often appeared in the Thursday night prayer, worship, and healing miracle meetings when people sang together in their heavenly language or during and after Friday night youth worship sessions. We kept a "book of records" in which we wrote the names and healing needs of people present and carefully chronicled the outcomes, personal testimonies, and visible transformations. We also recorded medically documented miracles as they came to our attention. In meetings where we saw God reverse congenital disease and erase cancers from bodies, we were very aware of the presence of angels.

In one very tragic case, a six-year-old girl from the congregation named Vivian contracted bladder cancer (probably due to uranium dust). In this case, our constant prayer and the specialist medical treatment that we raised money to finance did not have the desired result and our beloved Vivian passed to glory. However, what was beautiful was that in the final weeks of Vivian's life she would describe to me and to her parents how she kept being visited by angels. They would come regularly to her bedside and she talked of them as if they were her close friends. Despite being ravaged by disease, whenever she described the angels her face lit up with joy and delight.

Though the angels often appeared in dreams and visions (and at times in Bethlehem as electrical winds), in Baghdad they were almost always visible to the physical eye. Often, they appeared as sheets of light or blazing, glowing orbs of light, and at times we saw gigantic radiant men with faces of translucent light. Usually they seemed to have both wings and arms; they were always smiling but they did not speak. They were dressed in blazing white garments and they were all different in size and facial morphology, though they were always huge. Certain of them became familiar, recognizable faces that would reappear in different places. Their appearances always inspired deep joy, reverence, mystery, and awe and it seemed as if they felt welcome in our midst.

Still now, my Iraqi people in Jordan (as well as now in other nations) continue to reminisce about the angels as they were such an integral part of our world. Just last year before going to teach my sessions at the Bethel School of Supernatural Ministry in Redding, California, I was with my team, and one of my Iraqi families who emigrated to LA came to visit us in the hotel. As we gathered round the table, the first thing they talked about was the angels. My UK colleagues were eager to know more, and with great eagerness my people answered all their questions and gave detailed descriptions of the angels in our midst. Again, just last year I was at a Messianic Jewish conference in Chicago (currently home to more Iraqi Christians than anywhere else in the world) and was visited by one of the teenage girls who had emigrated there from Baghdad. Once again, she talked with my team, and at one point when reliving her sacred moments she described seeing the angels as "seeing Santa Claus for the first time" because of the "excitement" and because of the feeling of "not being forgotten." I sat with tears in my eyes as I heard once again the descriptions and witnesses of those whose tired, bereaved, yet joy-filled eyes had beheld the glory.

Often, the angels would stay around for periods of ten minutes and would surround and watch us worshiping. We felt extremely guarded and reassured by their presence and it was clear that they were protecting us. Central to the secret glory zone is angelic protection.

> *For you have made the Lord, my refuge, even the Most High, your dwelling place. No evil will befall you, nor will any plague come near your tent. For He will give His angels charge concerning you, to guard you in all your ways. They will bear you up in their hands, that you do not strike your foot against a stone* (Psalm 91:9-12).

Reflections

I wonder whether it was corporate, faith-filled worship that attracted the angels or whether it was the potential retaliation of enemy forces against our worship that was the reason for their being stationed in our midst. Maybe it was both. What I do know is that we were a courageous community stationed within a raging physical and spiritual battle and protected by guardians from another realm. I appreciate the rendition of the eleventh chapter of Hebrews by the authors of *The Passion Translation* as it best translates the original Greek reference to "pulling armies from another realm." This speaks to me of the magnetic attraction that faith in Jesus creates. I have observed the simple fact that steadfast faith in a perfect God attracts Heaven.

> *It was faith that shut the mouth of lions, put out the power of raging fire, and caused many to escape certain death by the sword. In their weakness their faith imparted power to make them strong! Faith sparked courage within them and they became mighty warriors in battle, pulling armies from another realm into battle array* (Hebrews 11:33-34 TPT).

Though we will never fully understand the mysteries of the angelic realm, the Bible is clear that their role is crucial to all aspects of Christ's redemptive work and the restoration of all things. Angels were intimately involved in the birth, life, death, and resurrection of Jesus. They are released by and attracted to divine sovereignty and majesty, and their role is to perform the will of Him who is sovereign. It is also clear throughout scripture that they relate to war, military activity, worship, protection, authority, commissioning, divine assistance, communication, fortitude, and deliverance.

> *Are they not all ministering spirits, sent out to render service for the sake of those who will inherit salvation?* (Hebrews 1:14)

Prayer

Father, I thank You for the increase of angelic activity that we are seeing in this hour. I pray that as we continue to worship, release Your word with authority, and submit to Your sovereign will, we will know the presence and ministry of angels in increasing measures. For all those who desire a greater sensitivity to and awareness of this realm, I ask that You answer the prayers of their heart by opening their eyes and sensitizing their spirits to angelic activity in their life.

Note

1.   Joshua Mills, *Moving in Glory Realms* (New Kensington, PA: Whitaker House, 2018), 109.

CHAPTER NINE

THE GOD WHO GOES BEFORE US

But be assured today that the Lord your God is the
one who goes across ahead of you like a devouring
fire. ...The Lord himself goes before you and will be
with you; he will never leave you nor forsake you.
—DEUTERONOMY 9:3; 31:8 NIV

MANY OF US RECITE KING DAVID'S WORDS FROM PSALM 23
and understand that divine glory follows us and we know that
we can experience this glory as a present reality. *"Surely goodness
and lovingkindness will follow me all the days of my life"* (Ps. 23:6).
However, we often fail to understand that the glory goes *ahead* of
us as well as *behind* us. The glory leads and the glory follows just as
it did for the people of Israel in the wilderness.

The apostle Paul states in Ephesians 1:23 that He is the one *"who fills all things everywhere with himself"* (NLT). I believe this includes not just people but atmospheres and physical spaces. In Baghdad, we saw spaces literally filled with His protective presence. Spaces that were filled with evil intent and that had been marked out for death and destruction became places of His presence. In my own high-risk quests of trying to reach people in dangerous places, the enemy was too late because God had gone before me.

In one experience, I planned to visit some members of my church who lived in Baghdad Jadida, which was an extremely dangerous part of the red zone. I was in the church gardens praying for confirmation when an angel gave me the confirmation that I required. As I mentioned in the previous chapter, the angels rarely spoke to us; they just seemed to surround us, strengthen, and protect us and make us fall more in love with Jesus. However, on this one occasion, a very large angel whose face I was familiar with (as he often appeared during worship) reappeared and looked straight at me giving me a clear instruction by signaling to me with his hand. He was pointing in the direction of Baghdad Jadida and summoning me.

Jadida means "new," but ironically it was one of the most derelict and downtrodden areas of Baghdad. It was full of trash heaps, burned-out neglected areas, dirt tracks, and empty football fields with no grass. There was an unbearable stench that filled the area due to the open sewers, which were some of the most vile and grotesque sights to see. It was around the year of 2008, not long after the coalition had departed, and when there was a lot of civil unrest as various faction groups were arising. During this year we saw the prelude to the anarchy that would later dominate the city. It was one of the most dangerous areas in the red zone, and my security did not want to go.

I eventually persuaded the military to accompany me and allow me to go as I wanted to visit certain Christian families and pray for those who were sick as I did on each regular visit. These particular families were some of the poorest of the poor. I cannot even describe to you the appalling and disgusting conditions in which they lived.

> *Then the King will say to those on His right, "Come, you who are blessed of My Father, inherit the kingdom prepared for you from the foundation of the world. For I was hungry, and you gave Me something to eat; I was thirsty, and you gave Me something to drink; I was a stranger, and you invited Me in; naked, and you clothed Me; I was sick, and you visited Me; I was in prison, and you came to Me." Then the righteous will answer Him, "Lord, when did we see You hungry, and feed You, or thirsty, and give You something to drink? And when did we see You a stranger, and invite You in, or naked, and clothe You? When did we see You sick, or in prison, and come to You?" The King will answer and say to them, "Truly I say to you, to the extent that you did it to one of these brothers of Mine, even the least of them, you did it to Me"* (Matthew 25:34-40).

Frankly, one would not even wish for the least of one's animals to live in the squalor and filth that these faithful believers lived in. Many of the younger ones were disabled and deformed due to an abnormally high level of congenital disease. It would seem that this was often due to the effects of depleted uranium (but also due to the shortage of Christians and the resulting degree of intermarriages, such as people marrying their second/third cousins or such like). The people were in the worst conditions imaginable, and it was my mission to minister the love of Jesus to them as regularly as possible.

The journey to Jadida usually took two hours; however, we were stuck in the heat in a "sheep jam" and the traffic came to a standstill. It was frustrating to be blocked by sheep, but for thirty minutes this was the case. Traffic jams and tank blockades were tedious enough, but congestion caused by sheep was somewhat more challenging to accept. The soldiers who had agreed to accompany me were becoming increasingly vocal and impatient and as the vehicles were not moving, they felt more vulnerable to attack. The sheep jam continued right to the entry point of Baghdad Jadida, and we became completely trapped by the sheep.

As I sighed with impatience and began to think, "Why Lord?" an enormous explosion went off inside the area, killing around twelve people. There was terrible bloodshed and some of the sheep were also killed. Had we been just a few meters further, we would have definitely been killed, but God had used the sheep-jam to save us. The great Shepherd had gone ahead of us; the glory zone had traveled with us. Most people would have turned back immediately at a scene like this. The explosive was an IED and there was never a guarantee that more devices were not waiting to explode beneath abandoned cars. However, I knew my God had gone before me, and I refused to turn back. Just as I was gathering my thoughts, the angel who had summoned me and signaled to me back at the church reappeared right there at the edge of the city. I was overwhelmed with joy and relief to see him as he summoned me forth. I entered Jadida with hope in my hand, bread and wine in my communion case, and faith in my heart.

When I arrived at the dilapidated homes of the families, prayed, blessed them, and shared communion with them, I felt an unusual sense of God's presence. It was only then that I saw the angel in the home with me; my assistant saw him too, and he had followed us into the house that we entered. As I write this, I have tears in my eyes because God is just so good. The angel's visible presence was radically empowering and deeply reassuring. I felt that sense of "weighty" glory where one feels completely overshadowed by the light and peace of Jesus. I knew the Father had commissioned His angel to accompany me, and I knew that He Himself had gone before me.

> *You will not leave in a hurry, running for your lives. For the Lord will go ahead of you; yes, the God of Israel will protect you from behind* (Isaiah 52:12 NLT).

There are countless stories that I could tell of God's intervention in times of great challenge. I remember two of my teenagers going out to get pizzas after one of the youth gatherings. Just minutes after they left the pizzeria, the entire restaurant was blown up. Had they not left when they did, they would have instantly lost their lives.

Another of my young Iraqi boys, David, was used instrumentally by God during my time living in the green zone in a high-security compound surrounded by guards. I had a major meeting that night with certain Iraqi ministers and other key leaders in order to discuss potential approaches to reconciliation and strategies for setting up interfaith dialogues. David sensed God saying that I should not attend the meeting. I ignored him and prepared to go, but he lay down across the door and would let not me pass. He was a tall, strong, robust young man, and this was not a joke—he was serious. He said he was sure of what he sensed in his heart and stayed blocking the door for over an hour. Later, when I called the Iraqi leaders and apologized for my non-attendance at the meeting, I learned that the entire team from the green zone had just been caught up in a major explosion and had all been killed outright. Words of knowledge are powerful, and often the younger people hear God the most accurately.

We must all develop an unhindered friendship with God and a sensitive, discerning spirit so that we hear Him when He speaks. I learned this early on in Baghdad. During one church service I became acutely aware in my spirit that a certain inoffensive-looking, smartly dressed man with a calm, composed demeanor needed to be instantly removed from the church building. There was no obvious exterior indication that the man's presence was sinister, yet during worship my spirit was in a state of deep unrest. I quietly spoke to my security guards and asked that the man be removed. The man was escorted out of the building and handed over to the Iraqi army who discovered that he was wearing a suicide belt around his waist that was packed with explosives.

We may not all live in a war zone, but the world is a dark place and we must all cultivate sensitivity to His voice and to the prompting of His Spirit. This comes from friendship with Him. We must walk in constant recognition that He is counsel, He is strength, He is revelation knowledge, He is understanding, He is wisdom, He is the reverent fear of the Lord, and He is the bold Spirit that declares Jubilee and proclaims Jesus. His resource is inexhaustible, and we must learn to walk hand in hand with Him.

Another powerful memory I have of God going literally before me and filling the space ahead of me relates to the only time in my adult life when I would say I experienced fear. It was around the year 2005-2006. A fortnight previously, I had been in the US where I was speaking at All Nations Church with my good friends Mahesh and Bonnie Chavda. It was a glory conference lasting several days, and the atmosphere of God's glory was thick throughout the conference. It came as waves over the entire gathering and many miracles and encounters were taking place.

At the end of the conference, as I was about to leave and return to Baghdad, Mahesh gave me one final hug and stuffed an unusually large sum of several thousand dollars cash in my jacket pocket. All Nations Church has always been generous supporters of our work in Iraq, but I have to say that this was an unusually large sum of money, and Mahesh assured me that God had told him to give this exact amount. I was extremely grateful for it, and on returning to Baghdad I placed the cash in a money belt that I wore around my waist beneath my body armor when moving around between zones.

Two weeks later I was working on a hostage negotiation case, attempting to rescue a group of Brazilian security staff. They were all former military men and experienced in dealing with kidnappings, but not of this extreme nature. After extensive investigation, my team and I managed to track down the kidnappers, and as confidentiality was critical to success we did not disclose details of the location to anyone other than my private driver who also acted as one of my bodyguards. My other group of bodyguards followed us in a separate vehicle up to a certain point. After this point, I journeyed alone with my driver toward the location, which was in a very dangerous suburb.

The kidnappers had no intention of negotiating and they were violent men. Holding my arms behind my back, they led me to an empty, dilapidated house. They threw me aggressively through the door of a very dark room and thrust me to the floor. I fell to the ground onto a hard, concrete surface and I was in a lot of pain. There was no light at all in the room, and I could sense the presence of evil.

After several hours, I realized that I still had my phone, and though there was no signal I used the light as a torch to see around the room. Fear entered me as I saw chopped off fingers and toes scattered all over the floor. I cannot even describe with vocabulary the deep dread that I felt in those moments as the light from my phone exposed the unspoken tortures of many yesterdays. Would I be the next victim? What would they do to me? Where was God within this sinister darkness? How much battery was left on my phone? How would I manage with no water? What would happen to my beloved wife and my boys? I was desperately thirsty, hurt, and bruised. Having been pushed so violently to the ground, my body felt terribly weak. As I sat in the darkness, I prayed, sang in my heavenly language, and wept with my head in my hands like a child.

There was just one music track on my phone at that time, and it was by a Jewish friend called Roni Shavit. I had known Roni since the day she was born. She is a highly talented musician, and I would often go to her family home and listen to her play, as her music always ministered great peace to my soul. By the age of sixteen, Roni became the official pianist in the Jerusalem Symphony Orchestra. I had been so overwhelmed by her stunning rendition of Beethoven's Piano Concerto no.2 in B-flat Major I recorded it live on my phone from Jerusalem, and, as I had literally no other music on my phone in those days, it became my "personal lullaby." It uplifted me on long journeys and in endless queues at check points.

There in that dark room, the phone that had given me light gave me sound, and as the room filled with this dynamic concerto I felt instantly fortified and could feel God's presence surround me like a blanket. Fear began to leave me, faith welled up in my heart, and I knew that somehow I would be liberated; somehow God would intervene. Somehow I would survive to tell you this story.

In those days, I always traveled with emergency money around my waist, and fortunately they had not searched me. I had totally forgotten that I had added Mahesh's large bundle of cash, and it was still there in addition to what had already been in there. This gave me enough cash to pay my captors for my own release and I managed to walk away a free man. There is absolutely no way I would ever consider carrying that amount of cash on me, but am I glad that Mahesh heard so accurately from God in the atmosphere of the glory two weeks before! Once again, God had already gone ahead of me, from the glory in North Carolina to a dark, death-filled room in a dangerous derelict of Baghdad. The zone had traveled with me; He had gone ahead of me and filled the sinister space with His rescue solutions. Everything I needed was already with me, and most of all, His glory was in me. The dark room had become filled with the protective and peace-filled presence of He "who fills all things everywhere with Himself."

As I mentioned at the start of this chapter, His goodness *is* His glory, it is the outflow of His nature. Divine goodness does not just follow us, it goes ahead of us.

The number of Iraqi bodyguards allocated to travel with me was thirty-five. This was the most common number for an Iraqi military section, usually the size of two squads. Military trucks called army "Bradleys" traveled behind, ahead, and one at each side, so I was always surrounded. There were also three or four military suburban trucks that accompanied us. Most of my bodyguards were God-fearing Christians, and all were passionate about my protection. I wore body armor consisting of a bulletproof vest, a helmet, military eye-protection glasses, and on many occasions this armor preserved me. Everywhere I traveled, my thirty-five armored bodyguards accompanied me, and very rarely did less than thirty-five turn up for duty.

I will always be deeply grateful to those thirty-five willing ones who accompanied me to the most dangerous of places, taking enormous risks in order to enable me to reach my people. Even when common sense said "no," they risked their lives to protect me and had unwavering faith in God. Recently when reminiscing and thanking God for my thirty-five men, I was led to Psalm 35.

> *Contend, Lord, with those who contend with me;*
> *fight against those who fight against me. Take up*
> *shield and armor; arise and come to my aid. Brandish*
> *spear and javelin against those who pursue me. Say to*
> *me, "I am your salvation" (Psalm 35:1-3 NIV).*

The most powerful revelation of God that David had was that He is the God of armies, He is the God who goes before us, He is the God who fights on our behalf, and He is the God who is at all times victorious.

We must have a fresh revelation of the majesty, sovereignty, valor, and fearsomeness of God. The earth quakes and trembles at the sound of His name. It was in meditating on Psalm 35 that I saw with renewed lenses the Warrior-God armored with His own light. We too must partake of this armor.

> *The night is almost gone, and the day is near.*
> *Therefore let us lay aside the deeds of darkness, and*
> *put on the armor of light* (Romans 13:12).

Although I wore physical military body armor, it was the armor of light, the presence of the glory that covered, protected, and preserved me. The glory is impenetrable and unshakable; it protects and covers whoever chooses to abide in it because He *is* the glory.

> *Many are rising up against me. Many are saying of*
> *my soul, "There is no deliverance for him in God."*
> *Selah. But you, O Lord, are a shield about me, my*
> *glory, and the One who lifts my head* (Psalm 3:1-3).

I know with certitude that this heavenly armor of light combined with the guiding voice of Holy Spirit and the protective presence of angels preserved my life more than military armor. No fiery dart of the enemy could pierce it. Consider the apostle Paul's famous description of the believer's armor from Ephesians 6:14-17:

> *Stand firm then, with the belt of truth buckled*
> *around your waist, with the breastplate of*

righteousness in place, and with your feet fitted with the readiness that comes from the gospel of peace. In addition to all this, take up the shield of faith, with which you can extinguish all the flaming arrows of the evil one. Take the helmet of salvation and the sword of the Spirit, which is the word of God (NIV).

I believe that to truly wear this armor is to literally cloak oneself in power and luminosity. It is enables us to live permanently in the "glory zone." When we wear this armor and sharpen our swords with "the word of our testimony and the blood of the Lamb," we stand as the greatest military force the earth has ever seen. Whether in villages and cities or nations, true kingly and priestly ministry can only be administered by an army of people walking in divine truth garmented in the armor of light just as it was for those spiritual warriors whom Paul was exhorting in Ephesus. Divine light is divine strength; it is a light that fortifies and protects. Each part of the armor to which Paul refers in Ephesians 6 is a part of the armor of light that he refers to in Romans 13. This is the armor that the Warrior-God equips us with. The offensive power unleased through the wielded sword and the testimony of Christ declared, relies on the other defensive parts of armor being securely in place.

Psalm 35 not only reminded me of the invincibility of God but caused me to re-embrace the lightness and weightlessness of God's armor. Unlike heavy military armor, the armor from above is weightless, radiant, and not subject to gravity. We can leap and soar in this weightless armor; it is the armor of spiritual eagles.

Reflections

The armor of light brings illumination of our true identity as ones who are hidden in Christ. It also enables us to emanate a supernatural radiance that shines forth in the darkest of places. As we know, the very heart of the great commission is to dispel darkness. Wherever we are, we were designed to exude divine light. The ministry of Jesus is the ministry of the glory. It is the ministry that endures in the darkest of hours and stands undiminished by the horrors of the night. It is the ministry of light.

Prayer

Father, I thank You that You go before us and that whatever tragedies, catastrophes, disasters, crises, or daily challenges lie ahead of us we can be assured of Your presence. I thank You, Jesus, that Your desire is to "fill all things with Yourself" and that this includes the darkest of places. I pray that You give those reading a renewed awareness of the armor of light, a crucial armor that protects against the works of darkness and enables them to carry light, life, protection, and order into places of oppression and disunity. I bless the generation of warriors who are standing in Your strength. Fill them with courage, Lord, and bless them, I pray.

CHAPTER TEN

KINGDOM'S CHILDREN, CHILDREN'S KINGDOM

I HAVE HEARD IT SAID MANY TIMES THAT "THERE IS NO child-sized Holy Spirit," and I believe this is a revelation that many of us still need to walk in. We must never allow the need for simplification of complex subjects or sensitivity to age, cognition, and intellectual understanding to lead to unintentional (or, worse still, intentional) dilution of kingdom realities. The ministry of children as ministers to the Godhead, through worship, and as ministers to the rest of the Body of Christ, regardless of age, is possibly one of the most neglected ministries.

Conversely, many would agree that the faith of children—unhindered by cynicism, rational analysis, and catalogues of negative experiences—is often more active than that of their adult peers. However, in the spiritual realm there is no age just as there is no color, no gender, no distance, no size, no class. Miracles, signs, and wonders are no less the children's portion than they are the adults' portion. We must not be biased either way.

> *Behold, I and the children whom the Lord has given me are for signs and wonders in Israel from the Lord of hosts, who dwells on Mount Zion* (Isaiah 8:18).

To return to my original point, which is the powerful ministry of children, I have often found brilliant peacemakers, diplomats, prophets, evangelists, prayer warriors, and discerning "hearers" among the children.

Many have placed the focus of "children's ministry" solely on "tending the lambs" and the establishment of generational legacy. While these emphases are important and it is true that we must "raise up the next generation," we must not find ourselves trapped in the word *next*. The kingdom is for *now* not *next*, the glory is for *now*—the children are not simply the *next* generation to experience the glory, they are the *now* generation. The scriptures could not be clearer about the fact that the kingdom is theirs in the here and now. It is their inheritance and their portion *now* regardless of whether they are a newborn, a toddler, or a teen.

> *Then some children were brought to Him so that He might lay His hands on them and pray; and the disciples rebuked them. But Jesus said, "Let the children alone, and do not hinder them from coming to Me; for the kingdom of heaven belongs to such as these." After laying His hands on them, He departed from there* (Matthew 19:13-15).

The great call of Jesus saying "let them come to Me" is still echoing down the generations. Let the children step into the glory zone, let them experience the divine supernatural, let them feast at the royal banqueting table, let them drink from the fountain of life, do not push them away, for the kingdom is the children's kingdom and it is for them, right now.

One of my favorite miracles involving children is the feeding of the five thousand. The reason I am drawn to this miracle is not simply due to the extraordinary drama but because of its powerful demonstration of the kingdom being there for the children.

> *One of His disciples, Andrew, Simon Peter's brother, said to Him, "There is a lad here who has five barley loaves and two fish, but what are these for so many people?" Jesus said, "Have the people sit down." Now there was much grass in the place. So the men sat down, in number about five thousand. Jesus then took the loaves, and having given thanks, He distributed to those who were seated; likewise also of the fish as much as they wanted* (John 6:8-11).

I do not believe that the calling forth of this young boy with his bread and fish was a random selection, a token gesture to show that God could use the weak and lowly ones. Nor do I consider the main focus to be on legacy, raising up the next generation of young Galileans to experience what they could achieve if they became a faithful adult disciple of the Messiah. Rather, I see this whole event as a powerful demonstration and confirmation of the fact that everything that Jesus was teaching and illustrating—every sign, wonder, and miracle, every example of surrendering to the will of the Father and being a conduit of His glory—was inclusive of every age. Jesus stated that He only did that which He saw His Father do in Heaven, and this meant that whenever He spoke or acted, the culture, the values, the realities of Heaven were being intentionally released at that given moment of time in order to establish a new reality on earth. The reality being established here was multiple in terms of the magnitude of the miracle; however, for me, the primary reality is as much in the inclusion of the child as it is in the multiplication of resource.

During my time in Baghdad, this reality was so integral to my work, my ministry, my revelation of Jesus, and my physical and emotional strength. Along with the Mothers Union, the unshakable faith and relentless worship of the children became the greatest battle force. Often they were the greatest carriers and stewards of the glory and the most vigilant and attentive watchmen ("watch-boys" and "watch-girls") of the glory zone. Often I saw the raw power emanating from the faith-filled praise of children literally dismantle and dispel enemy forces.

> *From the mouth of infants and nursing babes You have established strength because of Your adversaries, to make the enemy and the revengeful cease* (Psalm 8:2).

The prophetic insight of the children was acute, and their discernment was often very accurate, particularly in the area of timings and dates. The children were immersed in a culture of expectation and were very involved in praying for the sick, and their faith was cultivated in the atmosphere of expectancy that existed among all of the people. There was a simplicity and purity in their great conviction that God was exactly who He said He was and the idea of "nothing happens when we pray" was simply not within their mindset or vocabulary. Their mindset was always one of "when we pray, something happens"—this was their natural environment.

The children often gave precise timings about healings that would happen. For example, when praying for the sick during the Sunday service, one young child said that God had spoken to him and that the person he was praying for would receive their full healing on the following Thursday. Sure enough, the person was completely healed the following Thursday. Often before their own youth meetings or at the start of a new week, the children would have heard from God regarding what was to take place and on which day. What I love about children is their powerful combination of sensitivity and boldness.

> *I will pour out My Spirit on all mankind; and your sons and daughters will prophesy, your old men will dream dreams, your young men will see visions* (Joel 2:28).

We should be encouraging our children to give their spiritual senses to the Holy Spirit and enable them to cultivate their ability to see, hear, discern, and know.

I believe we should do all we can to prevent their minds and hearts being cluttered by worldly distractions and addictions so that they can develop clear vision and acute spiritual hearing like that of Samuel who immersed himself in the presence of God.

One of the key young people during my early years of reconciliation work was a nine-year-old American Messianic Jew named

Yoshi Singerman. His family are close friends of mine, and during the delicate years of my attempts to bring together Israeli and Iraqi religious leaders, Yoshi was instrumental. Yoshi presented me with an inspirational idea for the religious leaders to meet in Cyprus. This was a new, original idea and it soon became clear that the Holy Spirit was breathing on it and that God had chosen this young boy to be a key in opening the door to the first-ever meeting between Israel and Iraq. This historical meeting was attended by the highest-ranking government officials, senior religious leaders, ayatollahs, imams, and chief rabbis. As a result of the meeting, long-standing dialogues were opened and common ground established as each party listened to the stories of the other. Each party affirmed at the end of the meeting that though they had arrived full of fear, they had felt it diminish. Initiatives were launched and centers for grassroots reconciliation between Jews, Christians, and Muslims were set up in Gaza, Baghdad, Jerusalem, and Tel Aviv. These are called "Mosaica centres" and still exist today.

Though not present in the meetings, Yoshi had a reconciliatory role between all the different religious and political delegate groups and warmed their hearts by interacting with them and treating them as friends. Yoshi was completely unintimidated by his age and liaised with Arabic and Hebrew translators with confidence and kindness. Above all, he was a devout intercessor who helped his father run a 24/7 prayer room directly above the conference room where the meetings were held. I have no doubt that the relentless prayer of this young boy and his father, on my behalf, released the wisdom of God into the situation and enabled us to reap favorable solutions on every level.

Since those glory years in the war zone of Baghdad, the Christian Iraqi children from my congregation who currently reside in Jordan still remain on the front line of executive decisions. One such decision was the agreement to completely discard their denominational labels and to be known simply as "Massihi"—followers of the Messiah.

The school itself was the answered prayer of a young boy called Mario whose father had been shot by ISIS. On crossing the border into Jordan, Mario prayed for a school as Iraqi refugees have no rights to Jordanian education, welfare, or employment; they are only permitted to take refuge in the country. Later, on arriving in Jordan myself, I went to give financial support to his family and asked Mario if there was anything else that I could do for him. I had already agreed to be his "daddy" and to help him, his mother, and his sister as much as I could. In response to my question, Mario raised his head looked at me with eyes full of expectation and told me he had been praying for a school and believed God was going to provide one. This was a huge step of faith even for me. We gathered a group of children together and worshiped on a hillside ridge overlooking Amman. We prayed only for a short time; the rest of the time was spent in praise and worship. Within three weeks God moved on our behalf and the new school opened. I was put in contact with Father Khalil, a priest from Bethlehem who was working with the Iraqi refugee community in Jordan. He offered us free use of the Latin church and school facilities, and we created a team of personnel and administrative support. All this took place within three weeks. It was the absolute provision and orchestration of God. After three more months, all of the children had smart, fully tailored uniforms, and we began the process of restoring a sense of dignity, identity, and stability to the traumatized.

It sounds impossible to think that a school could be up and running within three weeks of a child's prayer. Yet this is the nature of the Father. He cares tenderly for His children, and wherever His name is glorified, His activity is seen because that which we focus on, we attract.

> I have learned through my life that though upon this earth we will never experience divine glory in its fullness, we can have a taste of it in advance. I believe this because I know that the glory all rests on one person and His name is Jesus. Personally, I have found that in my daily worship, in meditation and ministry to the refugee community, I experience the person of Jesus every day and every day I have a foretaste of His glory. In my work, there is a sense of overwhelming joy, divine reward, and at times, a sense of bliss that comes from His nearness.
>
> —FATHER KHALIL-JAAR,
> Director of "Messengers of Peace" and
> Head of Marka School for Iraqi Children

Another example of a child's unusual prayer being answered is that of a nine-year-old boy called Youssef. I had been teaching on the Fatherhood of God and reminding the children to be specific in their prayers and not just pray for peace and justice. I encouraged them to each ask God for something and I called one boy forward and asked him to share with me what he had prayed for. He told me that he had asked God for a Burger King; this was his dream as he walked past the signs and billboards each day to school and longed to be like the Jordanian children whose parents could afford to buy burgers and fries. I smiled at him and assured him that God had heard his prayer. The very next day, a group of Americans from Los Angeles who were on a tour of Jerusalem and Jordan came to visit the school. After taking a tour of the school and attending an assembly, the Americans said that they would like to arrange buses to take the children all to Burger King for a treat. Youssef was truly overwhelmed that God had answered his prayer. We must always remember that He is a good, kind, intimate Father.

> *Or what man is there among you who, when his son asks for a loaf, will give him a stone? Or if he asks for a fish, he will not give him a snake, will he? If you then, being evil, know how to give good gifts to your children, how much more will your Father who is in heaven give what is good to those who ask Him!* (Matthew 7:9-11)

Several years ago, when my good friend Rodney Howard-Browne was talking to leaders about their need to "see" the love of God, he turned to me and said, "Andrew, you have seen the love of God in the eyes of the children." This remark was so true, for I literally saw glory in the eyes of the children. One of the greatest virtues that marks the Iraqi children is their capacity for radical forgiveness. That is to say they have openly and publicly affirmed their forgiveness of those who have perpetrated the most heinous of crimes. They have been able to forgive those who have brutally killed and tortured their loved ones. They say that they are able to do this because they "want to be like Yesua" ("Jesus" in Arabic).

A profound sense of empowerment arose from the ability to give to one's enemies a gift that they do not deserve. Such acts and statements can only come from a place of true revelation. I always emphasized the need to ask God to empower us to love our enemies. I taught my people that when they cannot forgive, they must ask Jesus, the "forgiver" inside of them, to reach out His arms of mercy from within them toward the person who needs forgiving.

What was notable about the children was their capacity to forgive. During the war, several children whom we could not reach were collapsing from hunger as they did not have the physical reserves that the adults had. Others were venturing out to find close friends buried in piles of decomposing bodies around the checkpoint area on the bridge that crossed the river Tigris. Usually scenes like this were due to airstrikes. Bodies were found in common graves where stray dogs would eat them and sometimes relatives and friends were simply not found. Despite the haunting images that surrounded these children and despite the untold traumas that they have known, I have not yet met one child who has said they cannot forgive. Many during those years of brutal violence referred, in their own words, to Jesus being "with us in the explosions just as He had been with Daniel and his friends inside the fiery furnace." This was one of the most common comparisons they drew. Furthermore, each of them has in some way been touched by death and each knows the simple, profound truth that unlike Mohammed, Jesus, the innocent, holy Son of God, was brutally tortured for them and taught us to forgive. For many, it seems that they do not even know what unforgiveness is.

After refusing to renounce his faith in Jesus, one fourteen-year-old boy from my community named Youssef had oil poured over him by ISIS and was set on fire. His uncle was shot in front of him and his mother found him screaming and covered in flames. After four years of major reconstructive plastic surgery, initially in Iraq, then in Jordan, Youssef finally came to school. My team and I were there to welcome him and pray with him and the students held a solemn welcome assembly in the courtyard. The level of honor and reverence shown by the young ones as they stood together and welcomed in the latest hero was deeply moving. It was impossible to hold back the tears on seeing the condition of Youssef's skin and the obvious agony that he had suffered and continued to endure. When he initially regained consciousness, his mother and the Iraqi medical staff had refused to let him see himself in the mirror as it was too distressing. It took Youssef a long time to eventually gain the courage and confidence to leave the house. The extreme level of trauma spoke for itself, and on his first day at the school we just held him and let him rest his head on our shoulders as we wept in silence. Whenever I speak with Youssef he tells me that he has forgiven the terrorists for what they did, and he said this openly on a recent TBN documentary, quoting the words of Jesus with deep sincerity: "*whoever slaps you on your right cheek, turn the other to him also*" (Matt. 5:39).

Youssef had received a lot more than a punch in the face; he had literally been set on fire and had suffered immense agony. I worked with a few burn patients with third-degree/full thickness burns and fourth-degree burns in my medical days but never saw such an extreme case of intentional burning, nor will most doctors in their lifetime. Yet Youssef made a choice that his allegiance to Jesus meant he must forgive. This is just one of many stories and testimonies of children who have literally proclaimed to the cameras of the world that despite being tortured they have chosen to forgive.

Another virtue that emanates from the young Iraqi Christians is radical mutual love. The importance of "preferring the other" is dominant in Middle Eastern culture whether through hospitality, bestowal of gifts, communal sharing of gains, or sacrificial giving. During the drastic food shortages and later through the period of terrorist attacks, families would lean out of their windows and throw bread to neighbors and share the little they had as it was too dangerous to leave their homes. Children too sacrificed what they had to provide for the most vulnerable. The reality of Paul's words in First Corinthians 13 was lived out in a powerful way:

> *Love is patient, love is kind and is not jealous; love does not brag and is not arrogant, does not act unbecomingly; it does not seek its own, is not provoked, does not take into account a wrong suffered, does not rejoice in unrighteousness, but rejoices with the truth; bears all things, believes all things, hopes all things, endures all things* (1 Corinthians 13:4-7).

On arriving in Amman on one of my regular trips a few years ago, I noticed that Mariam, one of the young girls from my community in Baghdad, had cut off all of her long, dark hair and shaved her head. She explained that one of the other Iraqi girls (a close friend who shared the same name) had been diagnosed with leukemia. She had been diagnosed shortly after fleeing Baghdad and crossing the border into Jordan. Mariam's family had used the money that we had given them to help pay for the friend's chemotherapy treatment, but they could not afford to buy her a wig. The

Jordanian hospital had said that if hair was provided, they could make a wig without cost, so Mariam had given her hair as a gift to her friend. I was moved not only by this deep expression of intentional, resolute love, but by the fact that the girls shared the same name. This caused me to reflect once again upon their oneness in Christ. Stories such as this are examples of true agape love; they are the stories of children who lost relatives, friends, property, dignity, and educational opportunity. They are the stories of children who grew up in a war zone and lived through the horrifying acts of bloodthirsty terrorists. They are the stories of children whose future is fragile, children who stand empty-handed with hearts overflowing and alive with love—children who have nothing to give yet who still will give their hair.

As we said in Arabic every week at the start of our services: "Al-Hubb, al-Hubb, al-Hubb"—"We must love, love, love."

Reflections

Even in my most fragile state when I barely had stamina to walk, my desire was to be like Jacob who, with eyes of love, leaned on his staff and worshiped.

Let all of us, whatever we are suffering, reach out our arms to the children of our generation. My desire is to see them grow into mighty warriors and nation-changers. My greatest aspiration is that the children of today will truly go from glory to glory as they prepare for the return of King Jesus when the entire earth will be filled with His glory.

By faith Jacob, as he was dying, blessed each of the sons of Joseph, and worshiped, leaning on the top of his staff (Hebrews 11:21).

Prayer

Jesus, I bless the readers' children in Your name. I bless those who give their lives to work with children; I bless those with young ones in their world, and I extend a father's blessing to each child. I thank You that You are "the children's King," and I ask that You hold them, keep them, reveal Your rich affection to them, and let Your peace and joy overwhelm them. Father, I ask that You anoint every child represented and that Your purposes be accomplished fully in their lives. I ask that You attend to their needs and reveal Yourself to them though dreams, visions, miracles, signs, and wonders. I thank You, holy Father, for Your angels that guard them and for Your unconditional love poured out over and through them. Father, empower every parent and teacher to show the children who they are and whose they are. Show the children Your glory.

Chapter Eleven

Resurrection Glory

I am the resurrection and the life.
—John 11:25

In February 2017 while awaiting a flight to the UK in the airport lounge in Amman, I heard an audible voice reading this scripture. I turned to my colleague and asked her who nearby us was reading a Bible. She looked at me with a confused expression and asked what I meant. I asked her again who was sitting reading scriptures out loud and told her what was being read. "Andrew, it's silent up here, there is no one here, just a few businessmen on laptops. I heard nothing," she said. Still I insisted and sent my colleague to look around the lounge to see if anyone was near us reading their Bible. She got up and took a walk around the lounge and reported back to me, "Andrew no one was reading their Bible;

there is no one here, just a few businessmen. It must have been either Holy Spirit or an angel talking to you."

There are only a few occasions in life when I have heard a divine voice, audible to my physical ears and not an inner audible voice. This moment was one of them. As I contemplated what I has heard, the Spirit of Truth of Jesus reawakened a part of me and words of life resonated throughout my entire being, imparting hope and joy.

The reality of the resurrection power of Jesus framed my whole experience of the Glory in Baghdad. For all who believe, this truth is the foundational premise of both our activity and our aspiration. Our ministry is based on the knowledge that the same spirit that resurrected Jesus from the dead resides in us and our aspiration is that we may truly know Him and the power of His resurrection (see Rom. 8:11; Phil. 3:10).

We saw around eight dramatic resurrections amidst our community in Baghdad, and the beauty of them was that they did not all involve Christians families. Some were Muslim families who in desperation had chosen to reach out to Jesus.

Women Warriors in the Spirit

On one occasion, we saw a tiny, four-day-old Muslim baby die. The baby's body was taken to the hospital mortuary and placed in a fridge as the distraught family gathered around the very ill mother who had almost died in childbirth. A group of ladies from the Mothers Union who were one of the most active spiritual military prayer forces in Baghdad arrived at the hospital and without permission stormed into the mortuary. This would be impossible in a

Western hospital; however, such was the chaos and understaffing during that time in Baghdad, it was often easy to gain access into places that would normally be under very high security. The ladies located the baby in one of the fridges and carefully lifted the cold corpse into their arms, praying and crying in one accord for God to do a miracle and show His resurrection glory in their midst.

A few hours later, the living baby was returned to the mother and the mother's health was restored. Several miracles of this nature involved women; their fervent prayer and intercession was a dynamic force in our midst. Their worship was a fragrant, holy incense arising from within the smoke and ashes of war. This in itself is another example of divine reversal, because the dominant cultural Middle Eastern view of women as being inferior was being dismantled. Disempowerment was being subverted and overridden by a great demonstration of womanly authority and identity within the spiritual realm. I have seen throughout my work that where the ministry of women is honored and where the ministry of children is honored, the glory is all the more intense.

Reassembled

One of the most astounding miracles of simultaneous resurrection and rearrangement of body parts involved a young American embassy worker whose body was blown up during a road explosion. As car bombs continued to explode, I was called to the scene. The worker had been in a US military car and had been traveling through what we often referred to as the "transfer zone," which was the zone in between the high security green zone and the unprotected red zone.

We desperately prayed that God would preserve him; however, within ten minutes he had fallen unconscious and a little later he was confirmed medically dead with no pulse in his carotid artery, which takes blood to the brain. I could see from my medical experience that there was no hope for resuscitation; it was over. However, if there is one thing I have learned in this life—it is not over until God says it is over. In faith we reached to Heaven for a higher verdict, a better diagnosis, a different prognosis. Even in war zones, Heaven's perspective is not shaded by the sounds of scud missiles, the pools of blood, the perpetual bombs and explosions. With God all things are possible.

After we laid hands on the dead man, life suddenly came back to him and he stood up; his whole body having been reassembled and re-pieced. The emergency medical team arrived and looked very confused saying there was absolutely nothing wrong with him. How it all happened remains a divine mystery; what we did know was that we had a great invisible rescue force in our midst.

The Name of "Yesua"

On another occasion, a distraught Muslim man named Ahmed approached me and asked if his daughter could be treated in our clinic rather than at the university hospital (I had set up a clinic and a dentist within the church compound). I explained that she would get more appropriate treatment where she was and that there was nothing medically superior our clinic could do that would be more beneficial than the medical attention she was already receiving. He shook his head and wept in despair, saying, "Abouna, there is nothing they can do. My daughter is dying; she does not have long to live." Feeling his desperation and being moved by compassion, I knew there was nothing I could do but point him to the great High Priest in Heaven who loved him and his family with an everlasting love. I said to him. "I cannot help you, Ahmed, but return now to the hospital, and as you go just say the name of 'Yesua' over and over. Do not stop, just keep saying His name."

Ahmed left me and returned to the hospital only to find that in his absence his daughter had tragically died. As he tried to enter the room where she lay, he was greeted by sorrowful doctors who gave him the news explaining there was nothing more they could have done to keep her alive. Distraught and weeping, he rushed into the ward, lifted the linen sheet covering his dead daughter, held her in his arms, and helplessly cried out, "Yesua, Yesua, Yesua!" at the top of his voice. After a few minutes, his daughter gasped and sat up on his lap. Life had returned, hope had returned; Jesus, the great name upon whom he had called, had stepped on to the scene and the doctors stood back in a state of shock. Where Jesus is, resurrection is, where Jesus is, life is. I do not believe it was the desperate repetition of a name (that he did not truly know) that led this man to a divine miracle. I believe it was the merciful act of a God who heard the helpless prayer of a desperate man.

Ahmed came quickly to see me and tell me his news. His eyes beaming with joy, he told me he had followed my instruction and that after coming back to life his daughter regained strength quickly and asked for something to eat. As my thoughts diverted to the daughter of Jairus, I said, "Don't worry, my dear Ahmed, it's happened before!"

Reflections

One does not need to be in a physical war zone to be surrounded by death, brokenness, carnage, and morbidity. This morose landscape often characterizes our own personal lives. It may include relational breakdown, sorrow and bereavement, physical and emotional violation, mental depression. It may be that you feel suffocated by crises, caught up in a cycle of sadness, or incarcerated with no escape. It may be that you feel hope has been stolen and that you have been assigned to a lifetime of watching your dreams and aspirations die from behind prison bars.

Well, I am here to tell you that Jesus is hope, Jesus is resurrection, and Jesus is life. Fix your gaze on Him and lift His name above every circumstance. So often in impossible situations where I have followed the example of Ezekiel by declaring His Word and nature over the void, I have seen radical results.

If the prophets of old knew the resurrection power of the Creator as they did, how much more assurance we have in the knowledge of and partnership with the risen Son who took the keys of death, hell, and the grave.

The hand of the Lord was upon me, and He brought me out by the Spirit of the Lord and set me down in the middle of the valley; and it was full of bones. He caused me to pass among them round about, and behold, there were very many on the surface of the valley; and lo, they were very dry. He said to me, "Son of man, can these bones live?" And I answered, "O Lord God, You know." Again He said to me, "Prophesy over these bones and say to them,

'O dry bones, hear the word of the Lord.' Thus says the Lord God to these bones, 'Behold, I will cause breath to enter you that you may come to life. I will put sinews on you, make flesh grow back on you, cover you with skin and put breath in you that you may come alive; and you will know that I am the Lord'" (Ezekiel 37:1-6).

Prayer

Father, I thank You that You are the Creator of all life. Jesus, I thank You that You are the Resurrection and the Life. Where You are present, life is present. Holy Spirit, I thank You that You are the Spirit of Life, the very breath of God. I ask that as the reader lays everything aside and comes to a quiet place of rest in You, You breathe life into every void. I ask that You revive, reassemble, and resurrect everything that requires restoring and resuscitating. For those suffering autoimmune diseases and experiencing turmoil within their bodies, I release Your peace and harmony. For those with terminal illnesses, Father, let Your healing power flow through them right now. I sing the name of Jesus over every diagnosis of death.

CHAPTER TWELVE

THE GREAT NAME

AS WE SAW IN THE LAST MIRACLE, THERE IS GLORY IN THE *great name.* There is glory in "I am that I am." Glory is His name; it is the fullness of His personhood. "He is that He is." He is mystery and majesty. Ahmed knew neither the Savior nor the holiness of His name, but I did. In desperation he followed my advice and chose to place trust in a prophet who, according to his learning, is a good man but indisputably inferior to the prophet Mohammed. The result of saying the name of Jesus became a great sign to Ahmed, and my prayer to this day is that he re-encounters Him. Miracles always magnify the presence and power of Jesus because the glory *is* Jesus. It is the fullness of His present-ness.

Jews recognize the holiness in the name of God to such an extent that they refer to Him simply as *Ha Shem*—"the name." Though our revelations may differ, we have much to learn from the reverence of our Jewish friends and their ability to behold mystery.

Understanding that this great name (*Ha Shem*) applies equally to the Son and the Spirit, it enables us to embrace the Trinity more fully. Yeshua, the Son of God, is known by multiple names (Prince of Peace, Shepherd, Provider, Redeemer, Restorer, Friend, great High Priest) yet He is also a part of *the* name, the great "I am," the great singular, absolute name that is far above every other name.

During my time in the Middle East we saw the manifest power, authority, and glory of He who is the great name. On many occasions during the darkest hours, just whispering His name would release peace into the atmosphere. It flowed from a place of intimate revelation, not robotic repetition.

> The power is more than repeating the name; it is the nature of the name in you. It is the divine personality within, who has come to take up his abode in you.[1]

I do not believe that any of us across the world have even begun to truly understand the glory and power of His name. Yet in the war zone we learned the simple process of "hiding" in His name. When bombs and missiles are exploding around you and people are being kidnapped, beheaded, burned alive in cages, there is only one place to hide, and that it is in His name: *"The name of the Lord is a strong tower; the righteous runs into it and is safe"* (Prov. 18:10).

For me, to "hide in His name" is to find a place beneath His garments of white light where you can bury your head and hide away from the terror that surrounds you. I have experienced the unspeakable joy and the reality of hiding in His name. It is a strong tower and a lighthouse that overlooks but is not diminished by stormy seas. His name is itself a glory zone.

To walk with Jesus is literally to take a journey into the fullness of His name; to have Christ fully formed in us is to come to a point where we are able to live *out* of His name and all of the peace, power, and authority that it contains. The recognition of power and authority in Jesus' name was expressed not just by His disciples and those to whom He ministered, but by those who despised Him and envied His popularity.

Peter:

> *And on the basis of **faith in His name**, it is **the name of Jesus** which has strengthened this man whom you see and know; and the faith which comes through Him has given him this perfect health in the presence of you all...**by the name of Jesus Christ the Nazarene**, whom you crucified, whom God raised from the dead—by this name this man stands here before you in good health* (Acts 3:16; 4:10).

Rulers, elders, and scribes:

> *"The fact that a noteworthy miracle has taken place through them is apparent to all who live in Jerusalem, and we cannot deny it. But so that it will not spread any further among the people, let us warn them to speak no longer to any man **in this name**." And when they had summoned them, **they commanded them not to speak or teach at all in the name of Jesus*** (Acts 4:16-18).

Another Iraqi family that learned the power of this great name was the family of the grandson of General Nashbandi. General Nasbandi was the best friend of Air Vice Marshal Georges Sada who later became the director of the Iraqi Institute of Peace and served as my chief of staff. It was in 2004, just after the invasion, when the general's grandson named Ali, who was four years old, was being operated on for leukemia. In order to undergo a bone marrow transplant, he was taken to Israel for intensive treatment at the Hadassah Ein Kerem hospital. The treatment was funded by a Christian American charity that works in Israel and brings very ill patients from all of the Middle East to be treated by Israeli cardiac surgeons. I was at the hospital praying with my good friend Connie Wilson who was the assistant to Ruth Ward Heflin. I stayed intermittently with Connie and her husband General Bill Wilson for twelve years and had a room in their apartment overlooking the old city, which was my base for when I was in Jerusalem.

We fasted and prayed incessantly that God would do a miracle, and we all believed that Ali would survive. However, just as things were looking positive, they suddenly turned for the worse. As we stood praying around Ali's bedside and watched him dying, my medical experience enabled me to see that unless God intervened, we would lose him not within a day but within hours. Though the Nashbandi family were Muslims, I prayed earnestly in front of them that Ali would go to be with Jesus and to no other place. Connie also joined me fervently in prayer, and as we prayed we saw a thick layer of glittering gold dust suddenly land all over Ali's body. It was not perspiration; it was not some chemical leakage; it was bright dazzling gold dust that suddenly appeared all over his body. As this beloved four-year-old left this world, I believe that he passed from Jerusalem on earth to the Jerusalem above.

The gold all over his body had caused his parents to not only weep even more but to radically change their view on the God of Israel and their attitude toward the majesty and deity of Jesus. As I was praying and watched the gold appearing all over the boy's face and over his white hospital gown, his heartbroken parents repented from their hatred of Israel and the God of Israel. They said because the Israeli medical team had fought to save their son and the God of Israel had caused gold to land on him: "Israel is now our friend." Connie and I explained that Jesus, our God, lived His life as an Israeli Jew. We talked to them about Jesus and how we knew that Ali was with Him. They continued to weep in deep pain and wonder. Though the family did not say that they had converted or even that they intended to convert, they had a profound change of heart toward the name of Jesus and toward Israel. Why was this? Ultimately it was because they had experienced the great name and the rich sovereign majesty that flows from that name.

We often talk of signs, wonders, and miracles; they are a natural experience for those who are followers of the Most High, but it is essential that we come to a true knowledge ourselves that Jesus Himself is the ultimate sign and He is the greatest of wonders. He is wonder-filled and overflowing with wonder, and He Himself is the greatest of miracles. Mary knew the reality of this as she carried Him in her womb; Simeon prophesied it; the Magi knew it; Galilee, Jerusalem, and Samaria witnessed it; and Abraham saw and rejoiced in it. The apostles walked in it!

When I reflect upon my experience of glory within the war zone, I like to think of "signatures, wonders, and miracles." This is because every sign for me is essentially a "signature." It is the master "signing His name," engraving His imprint on a person, a moment, a space, a situation. What do we know about signatures? They are unique; they hold authority, identity, and validation. Signatures are fresh, original, and authentic; they are owned by a single owner. They express legality, finality, and permission. Oh, how I love the great signatures of Heaven, the recognizable "signings" of God's name on events and on lives as He intervenes and creates, recreates, restores, and transforms. There is no joy greater than seeing and experiencing the divine signature of God being written into one's everyday reality. When you see the King's sovereign seal, the mark of the signet ring that follows the rising of the scepter, you see His glory, you see the enactment of His will. Just as the letters that Esther wrote bore the redemptive seal of sovereignty, so today our role is to rise up in faith, authority, royal identity, and intercession so that the King's signature becomes more and more visible and legible in our day. Reflect upon your own life—consider the moments when you saw the signature of the King on certain transactions, moments, and occurrences. Take a look in the mirror and consider the fact that you yourself bear the signature of the King.

As I mentioned, there is infinite divine authority, identity, and capability inherent in His name as this name contains His full personhood.

As I mentioned in a previous chapter, not long after our refugee school was established, the children whose religious backgrounds and origins were a diverse mixture of Chaldean protestant, Syrian orthodox, Catholic, Assyrian, and Armenian made an executive decision to discard these titles. Just as they had been one in St. George's Baghdad, they wanted to be known in

Jordan as Massihi—followers of the Messiah. Their parents had already walked in this reality in Baghdad while still honoring the Christian traditions in which they had been raised, but now it was the children's turn to choose for themselves the name by which they wanted to be known. For me, the purity and simplicity of their desire contained a hidden power. It is the power of oneness in His name.

> *Holy Father, keep them in Your name, the name which You have given Me, that they may be one even as We are* (John 17:11).

These schoolchildren are proud to be followers of the Anointed One and (like many children) are quick to discard the categorizations and complex labeling mechanisms that adults are often socially conditioned to adopt, value, and rely upon. We must understand that there is no name worth carrying, no name worth defining oneself by other than the name of Jesus the Messiah.

I would like to tell you a story from my close colleague Father Khalil-Jaar, who now directs our refugee school and oversees many of my former Iraqi congregation currently residing in Jordan. When my staff asked him about his great, unshakable faith in God's faithfulness and provision, he told them this story:

> One of my most powerful lessons concerning the nature of God was given by a five-year-old boy. It was during a service in Zarqa, Jordan in 1994 during a kindergarten party of about eighty children. All the children were age four and five, and as part of the program for the event, one of the young boys gave a small speech to the audience. This little boy was very

lively and bold. He was so tender and courageous in the way that he spoke, he drew the hearts of the entire audience.

I was so moved by this young poet and the eloquence of speech that I called him aside at the end in order to reward him for his excellent work. On the table near me was a very large bowl full of sweets for all of the children to enjoy. As his reward, I called him to come to the table and I said he could dip his hands in the bowl and take as many sweets as he would like.

Suddenly this little boy who had been so bold and lively became very calm, quiet, and serious and I had to strongly encourage him again to take as many sweets as he wanted. Despite my encouragement he stood quietly and looked up at me earnestly, calmly refusing to help himself.

Well, I had never seen a child refuse to take sweets and chocolates before and this child was not usually timid, so I said to him again, "What is the matter, my little man? Come on, please, you must take as many as you want." He continued to refuse and then finally in a whisper so that no one else could hear he said: "But Father, my hands are so small and if you take them for me, I will get more because your hands are bigger and then it will be better for me."

Here at this moment I knew God was speaking to me. The wisdom of this young boy was imparting to me a lifetime of lessons on the importance of never relying on my own hands. I must always depend on the much larger hands and the infinite ability of the good, kind Father who stands in my place. If I could teach you one lesson it would be to never depend on your own capacity to acquire resource; you must always depend on your Father who is far superior and far more able.

When I consider this story, I reflect once again on the all-sufficiency of the Almighty and find myself humbled by the immense authority of His great name.

> *For this reason also, God highly exalted Him, and bestowed on Him the name which is above every name* (Philippians 2:9).

Why on earth would we want to rely on our smallness when we can benefit from His infinite magnitude? Why trust in our own ability, our own strength, our own authority when, just as this young child did, we can calm down, compose ourselves, realize our ineptitude, raise our heads, fix our gaze, and call upon the name of the Lord?

Reflections

I once heard a speaker say that "to live a life with Jesus is to embark on a pilgrimage into the fullness of His name." I have learned that this is true, for His name is so mysteriously and majestically infinite, so multifaceted, so unfathomable. His name is not a title or a label, not a slogan or an epithet. His name is like a gigantic blazing star that never collapses but is ever-exploding with divine life. His name does not refer to what He is *called* but to who He *is*.

A person whose surname is Silversmith may never work with silver, but this is not the case with Jesus. He *is* peace, life, living water, living bread, resurrection, counsel, direction, freedom, friendship, salvation, healing, majesty. Like His Father, He is that He is. Oh, that we may know the glorious and mysterious depths of His sovereign name.

Prayer

Father, I ask that every person reading will learn what it is to journey into the reality of Your name. Open their eyes to new dimensions of Your nature as they embrace the fullness of Your name. I thank You that You are the all-sufficient one and that You are attentive to those who call upon You. I ask, Spirit of understanding and revelation, for fresh vision and insight into the matchless wealth and authority of the name above every name.

Note

1. Wigglesworth, *The Anointing of His Spirit*, 125.

CHAPTER THIRTEEN

PEOPLE OF COVENANT

GOD IS A COVENANTAL GOD AND THE FATHER OF A COVE-
nant family. It is the revelation of covenant identity (in relation
to both sonship and covenant family) that empowers the glory in
our midst. The realm of God's presence is the private, legal, exclusive domain of the covenant-maker and the covenant-keeper. Only
those in covenant with Him can experience the judicial benefits
of this irrevocable covenant. The fact is, the glory zone is in fact
the *covenant zone*. It is the zone into which the young shepherd
boy David stepped. He was a righteous young man who walked
in alignment with the purposes of God. He was fully armored
in light, garmented in glory, and empowered by a revelation of a
covenant-keeping God. David was quick to see that the despicable
giant who stood before his nation was out of covenant, he was an
uncircumcised Philistine, his armor was non-existent, he was void
of authority, he was "out of zone." Goliath was no more than a grotesque puppet facing a *son of the covenant* whose gaze was set on

the Almighty and who knew the fearsome and awesome reality of being joined to the God of Israel. The story was always one that the children in my congregation loved to act out. Due to my height, I was the giant whom they would slay and behead. It was a drama that they became attached to and a perfect way to immerse them in the truth that they, like David, were "children of covenant."

As we know the birth, ministry, death, crucifixion, resurrection, and ascension ministry of Jesus as High Priest and King opened up the greatest pathway of glory that creation will ever witness. The journey of Jesus as Alpha and Omega, the Lamb slain before the foundation of the world to be the eternal "new and living Way" is all about covenant. The shed blood and the great divine exchange form the parameters and limits of the glory zone. One cannot legally enter the zone if one is out of covenant with Him. The full legal and beneficiary rights to the experience of His glory are only for those whose names are written in the Lamb's book of Life, for those who have accepted Jesus the Messiah as their eternal living sacrifice.

The great victory of the cross and the sharing of the bread and wine, which I often to refer to as the "covenant meal," was part of our daily reality in Baghdad. There was bread and wine with me almost all the time, and partaking of it was a constant, integral part of our day. It was an expression of worship, solidarity, victory, and divine covenantal oneness with God and with each other. I am a great believer in being intentional with our choice of locations and sharing of this covenant meal outside of the four walls of the church building, whether in gardens, at riversides, or in people's homes. This is the way the early church operated, and there are many lessons that we can learn from the intimacy, fellowship, and mutual hospitality that strengthened collective identity.

One of the most unusual yet powerful communion gatherings I had was beneath Saddam Hussein's Victory Arch. The arch was designed by Saddam after the Iran-Iraq war as a celebration of Iraqi victory. The monument consists of a huge pair of hands (which the dictator had modeled using his own hands) that emerged from the ground brandishing two swords. The swords were partly composed of metal from guns and tanks of Iraqi soldiers killed in the Iran-Iraq war. This monument became not only a sign of national victory but of the fierce dictatorial grip of the Saddam regime.

Due to the brutality and excessiveness of the dark, sinister regime that it symbolized, revolutionary gangs attacked it and attempted to destroy it as soon as Saddam fled and hid underground. During the time of Saddam's arrest leading up to his execution (and in the days thereafter), the monument became increasingly attacked and many people understandably called for its complete demolition. The arches were in the area of the green zone where military parades took place and the symbolism of authority, self-exaltation, enmity, and territorial dominion spoke for itself. It was thus with prophetic purpose and intentionality that we stood within the "dark" space directly beneath the dictator's arches and shared bread and wine. I purposefully gathered Christian diplomats, soldiers, international dignitaries, and congressmen to share communion together and to unitedly declare the presence of a higher authority. Together we stood on the enemy's territory in front of the emblem of a cruel, barbaric, self-exalting dictator and exalted the name of Jesus Christ. Together we declared that the power of His shed blood, the glory of His resurrection, and the authority of

His name were more powerful than the forces of evil at work in the land.

I believe that the remembrance and recognition of Christ's body goes beyond Jesus the Son of Man to the honoring of the body—the local, regional, national, and global church. I believe that covenant in this sense is not just vertical but lateral; it involves the recognition of covenant relationships from our homes to the nations. This recognition of our identity as *the body of Christ* places in us a desire to bless other people, regions, and nations as we meet as one. The honoring of the body of Christ must cause each part of the body to fight spiritually for the liberty and wholeness of the other and to declare the covenantal promises over each other. I am deeply blessed when I see church communities around the world reaching out their hands in prayer and declaration over other nations. I know of individuals and groups who share the covenant meal together over the internet from different nations in different time zones, and I believe that this is a powerful prophetic act.

We had countless experiences during these special times of sharing the bread and wine. We saw sorrow and grief lift immediately, fear flee instantly, indescribable joy fill the room, tears of gratitude and wonder being poured out. People often had visions as their spiritual eyes opened and those whose family members and friends were victims of violence and torture found supernatural grace and enablement to forgive their enemies. When I consider the level of violation and criminality that my people and I witnessed in Iraq, only deep, radical, supernatural forgiveness can work. When you know that inside of you there is a radical Forgiver who gave His own life to be the greatest human-rights lawyer the world will ever see, you realize that if you can somehow behold Him, allowing

His Spirit to move in you and His arms of forgiveness to reach out of you, you can forgive. The glory abolishes unforgiveness and it releases waves of mercy and love. When Jesus died and "led captivity captive," He was also leading unforgiveness captive.

As we shared bread and wine, trauma was often released as people came to a realization that Jesus carried trauma for them. We also saw miraculous healings both in larger church services and in small groups. I will always remember the day when dear Stephen got up and started to walk. Stephen was a lame boy who had never walked; he had suffered from cerebral palsy since birth. In youth meetings when talking to the teenagers, I would sit in my chair and the youth would sit around me in a circle either on the floor or in chairs. The circle was perfect for times of intimacy—they would hold hands in a circle while praying, and they loved to dance.

When Stephen was a young boy he would always come and sit between my feet while I was speaking at the Friday night youth meetings. He would crawl to get to me, or someone would help him get to me. It was almost like a little ritual that he had—this was his special place to sit and no one else was allowed to sit there. All of my people referred to me as "Abouna" ("Father"), and in Stephen's mind the special place to sit was in between Abouna's feet where he was guarded on each side by Abouna's very big shiny shoes.

The day that Stephen saw a miracle was one Friday evening during the sharing of the covenant meal. The youth, having already witnessed several dramatic miracles, decided to pray for him. They declared the resurrection power of the cross over Stephen and prayed with expectancy. This level of anticipation was natural as it was normal for them to see Jesus answer. Within a few minutes of them praying, suddenly Stephen got up and started to walk for the first time ever. He walked a little, and, as his legs gained strength, he ran straight up and down the aisle of the church. There was such an atmosphere of the glory in our midst that night. The youth were full of joy and passion as they watched Stephen receive his miracle and the power of the resurrected Christ activate his legs. My team and I had a reunion with Stephen and his family in LA last year when we were there at Bethel church. My colleagues were there to see the family crying with joy over us being reunited. Stephen's sisters began to describe life in Baghdad, and once again the miracles and the angels that came to the church gardens were the primary topic of conversation.

People often ask me how my people reacted to the supernatural. The truth is, it had almost become the norm. Just as suffering was the norm, the glory was the norm. The children grew up having visions of Jesus, prophetic dreams, words of knowledge, moments of divine intuition, miracles of healing, mysterious occurrences, and encounters with angels. The young people were more astounded when miracles did *not* happen than when they did. Their worship and their declaration of the healing and resurrection power of Jesus (especially through the breaking of bread) was so regular, so integrated, yet so passionate, radical, and raw, I believe it opened portals that released the miracle realm. They seemed to just *pull* on Heaven. The sense of harmony, fraternity, and oneness in Christ (across all ages) was refreshingly authentic, as was the love of the people for their God.

People also often ask me why I saw more of the miraculous in Baghdad than I have in the West. While I cannot explain it fully, I always propose two major reasons. First, there was such a pure, undistracted sense of expectancy arising from an absolute, unwavering belief in the goodness and sovereignty of God. The Iraqi people were passionate, expectant people; they were deeply proud of the God they worshiped. They felt honored to be followers of Yeshua and not of Mohammed; their identity and their allegiance to Jesus were treasures to them. They were people of resolve and perseverance, resolute and clear-minded about their faith. They were brave hearts, full of courage and tenacity, and there was a simplicity and a clarity about their walk with Jesus. The world of choices, options, doctrinal nuances, exegetics, denominational differences, and preferred styles that clutter our experience in the West was not the world they lived in. Their world was far from perfect, far from ideal; neither was their revelation necessarily fuller or deeper than those of other nations; however, they benefitted from a single-mindedness and an undistracted, unmaterialistic mindset. They profited from lack of options and they were passionate about worshiping the King. In some ways, "lack" became their greatest asset. Where our Western Sunday morning concerns may relate to bad weather, not getting our church parking place, someone taking our favorite seat, a technical hitch, or an acoustic problem, the Sunday morning concerns for the believers in Baghdad related to whether they would get to church alive and whether their friend who lived in the area of the most recent explosion would be would be alive and well in the congregation.

Second, as one teenage girl in my congregation responded when asked by an interviewer from *Voice of the Martyrs* why there was so much joy in the church when surrounded by such terrible atrocities: "When everything has been taken from you, Jesus is all you have left." We talk all the time about Jesus being "the center" but for many this is a theory not a reality. I agree with the response of Lina—who has now emigrated to Canada where she and her husband attend Catch the Fire Church, Toronto, and whose wider family is still in Jordan—"When Jesus is all you have, you realize He is all you need."

Reflections

When Jesus truly is our cherished possession and we know the joy of being in covenant with Him, we experience indescribable depths of joy that energize and sustain. We receive rich revelation, which in turn leads to deeper adoration. Of course, we can live within the materialism of the West and still be deeply in love with and reliant on Jesus. To suggest that we cannot would be absurd, especially when so many of those in Western churches are ministering to the suffering and the hurting precisely because they have such deep revelation of the majesty and all-sufficiency of Jesus. Wherever we live, the more undistracted and aware of His worth we are, the more we will see of His glory. The more unwavering and reverent our gaze is, the more we will see. The freer we are from inferior affections and empty vanities, the more "space" we will have for Jesus to fill.

> *And the church is his body; it is made full and complete by Christ, who fills all things everywhere with himself* (Ephesians 1:23 NLT).

Prayer

Jesus, I thank You for the glorious realties of the new covenant and I thank You that You are the promise-keeper. I pray that You would open our eyes anew to the magnitude of our inheritance in You. I ask for new revelations of Your all-sufficiency as You remove small perspectives and earthly mindsets and reveal the fullness of who You are. I thank You that Your desire is to "fill" all things with Yourself and to be "fully formed" inside each one of us. I ask that You saturate, infuse, and fill the atmosphere of every home represented by these readers and that as they partake of the covenant meal and share the bread and wine, their eyes (like those of Your early disciples) will see more of You and behold more of Your majesty.

CHAPTER FOURTEEN

MARTYRDOM AND ALLEGIANCE

ALLEGIANCE IS NOT A WORD I HEAR USED IN THE WESTERN church. It tends to be used more in relation to sports teams or to political parties, patriotic loyalty, and earthly monarchies than it is to King Jesus. Earthly allegiance is important, and we are told to honor those leading our nations, yet we need a greater understanding of how *allegiance* applies to us spiritually. The foundational reality of our calling as the body of Christ is related to our covenant with Him and His identity as the ruling, sovereign monarch, the King of all kings. Allegiance refers to "loyalty to the crown."

> *All the officials, the mighty men, and also all the sons of King David pledged allegiance to King Solomon* (1 Chronicles 29:24).

The word *allegiance* is related to the word stékó—"to stand." How can one "stand" in a war zone? The answer is we cannot unless we have given God full possession and rights to our lives and pledged exclusive allegiance to Him. As the apostle Paul states, we must become bond-slaves through our perpetual blessing of His name and our relentless testimony. The allegiant ones who are wedded to Him stand with valiant courage and praise through the pressure. They worship through the war. *"Therefore, let us offer through Jesus a continual sacrifice of praise to God, proclaiming our allegiance to his name"* (Heb. 13:15 NLT).

When I contemplate history there are always certain key figures who stand out due to the strength of their allegiance. There are thousands if not millions of stories told and untold.

During the Second World War, the German pastor, theologian, and anti-Nazi dissident, Dietrich Bonhoeffer was known for standing his ground in the face of Nazi tyranny. He raised the first voice of church resistance to the persecution of the Jews and defined allegiance well:

> Who stands firm? Only the one whose ultimate standard is not in his reason, his principles, conscience, freedom, or virtue; only the one who is prepared to sacrifice all of these when, in faith and relationship to God alone, he is called to obedient and responsible action. Such a person is the responsible one, whose life is to be nothing but a response to God's question and call.[1]

Eberhard Bethge, a student and friend of Bonhoeffer, recalls the eyewitness account of one of the Christian men who was present at the site of his execution within the Flossenbürg camp. This man was also a medical doctor:

> ...kneeling on the floor praying fervently to God. I was most deeply moved by the way this most lovable man prayed, so devout and so certain that God heard his prayer at the place of execution, he again said a short prayer and then climbed the few steps to the gallows, brave and composed. His death ensued after a few seconds. In the almost fifty years that I worked as a doctor, I have hardly ever seen a man die so entirely submissive to the will of God.[2]

How can one walk so confidently, courageously, and calmly into death? When I talk to families and friends of martyrs, I conclude that there must be an element of being hidden inside the King to whom we pay our allegiance—He who is standing and withstanding for us. I believe this is why Paul stated: "Christ in you, the hope of glory." It is the Christ inside of me that helps me stand and it is me being in Christ that helps me stand. Allegiance then comes from this revelation. It is all about 'stékó', standing firm. One cannot be allegiant to anything one does not trust or to anything one does not value. The greater the sense of being hidden in Him, the more I come to a knowledge of His nature. The more I know Him, the more I esteem and value Him. The more I desire to see Him, the more I see. The more aware I am of His majesty, the more empowered I am to love Him unto death. This empowerment to love unto death is, for me, the meaning of allegiance.

It was the reality of kingdom, kingship, and royal identity that I emphasized the most in my teachings in Baghdad. This emphasis was crucial due to the social, political, and spiritual climate of the day. I considered it part of my call to constantly remind my people of their sonship, their spiritual authority, and their royal connection to the King. For them allegiance was "loyalty to royalty" and the ability to stay faithful to the end.

Allegiance is commonly affirmed through the raising of flags and banners that display and represent the team, party, nation to whom one is allegiant. These emblems signify pride, identity, solidarity, and fidelity. Banners in ancient warfare moved in front of the host and determined the movements of the army. They consisted of a rigid pole with some solid ornament of bright metal on the top in order to catch the sunlight.

We see significant biblical reference, during times of war, to signal flags, battle flags, banners, and accompanying trumpet blasts. Banners are the billboards of kings, and spiritually they are the landscape of the war zone. It is our duty as citizens of the kingdom to raise the sovereign banner that has been given to us by the Father. *"You have given a banner to those who fear You"* (Ps. 60:4).

The execution site of Jesus released the fullest affirmation of allegiance and the most powerful raising of the Father's victory banner. What is this banner? It is love: *"He has brought me to his banquet hall, and his banner over me is love"* (Song of Sol. 2:4). The allegiance of Jesus to His father was crystallized through the full surrender of His own will. Spiritually, we can only wave flags and raise banners because Jesus was allegiant.

One cannot truly understand martyrdom without having a true revelation of kingdom and kingship. My children knew they were the children of a king who owned an invisible kingdom. It was not a Harry Potter fantasy kingdom nor was it a magical fairy-tale of a Disney paradise. The Kingdom of Heaven was as real to them as the bread they ate and more real to them than the war zone. How do I know this? Because I had children in my congregation who were beheaded and walked to their death singing, "Jesus loves me this I know." Again, as I reflect, I am reminded once again of the words of Dietrich Bonhoeffer: "To endure the cross is not a tragedy; it is the suffering which is the fruit of an exclusive allegiance to Jesus Christ."[3]

My children knew about the banquet hall and they knew that the King's banner over them was love. They and their families had pledged allegiance to the Lamb. They were not killed and slaughtered simply because they were caught up in a war zone; they were killed with intention because they refused to renounce their allegiance to the Lamb. Often the children were given time to reflect before responding to the choice of converting to Islam or dying—sometimes they were given just minutes, other times hours, but they held fast to the divine word hidden in their hearts and refused to break covenant with the Covenant-Keeper.

> *You have come to obey from your heart the pattern*
> *of teaching that has now **claimed your allegiance***
> (Romans 6:17 NIV).

Essentially what my congregation knew was that the Lamb's Book of Life was the King's Book of Life and that their names were inscribed in it. Many of my community (Iraqi Jews as well as Christians) were brutally tortured. Only one of our kidnapped church members ever returned, and after counting 1,127 people either dead or missing, I gave up counting. During the worst

155

attacks around 2010–2012 in Nineveh and Mosul, homes and businesses were burnt and ravaged by ISIS. The terrorists painted and sprayed images of the Arabic letter Nūn all over their properties. This symbol is equivalent to the letter N, and to the perpetrators it signified the word *Nassara,* meaning "Nazarene." Certain terrorists tattooed it on their victims (dead or alive) as an act of hatred and it became known as the Christian genocide symbol. This symbol of enmity was used throughout the Islamic world and was not dissimilar to the yellow star that Jews were forced to wear during the Nazi occupation.

Though denying His deity, Islamics considered Jesus a worthy prophet, so ISIS believed that by referring to Christians as "Nazarenes" they would "not be insulting a prophet." The perversion of this rationale was no less extreme than the ideologies that fueled Nazism. Many terrorists invaded properties, jeering violently while waving flags with the Nūn sign on it. These hate-filled murderers obliterated the whole infrastructure of Nineveh for a few years.

Today, my students wear the Nūn sign in the form of a small red and white badge as a remembrance of their journey. They wear this badge as a statement of collective pride; they are telling the world that they are proud to be associated with Jesus the Nazarene. Meanwhile, they continue to wave their Iraqi flags which state that "God is great," and to them these flags refer to the one true and living God. As they worship, they remember that they are His cherished possessions and ultimately the bearers of a superior flag—that of Jesus of Nazareth, their Redeemer and King. Once again, we are seeing dramatic divine reversal as the symbols and labels used for isolation and brutality become signs and emblems of pride and identity:

> *Thus says the Lord, "Let not a wise man boast of his wisdom, and let not the mighty man boast of his might, let not a rich man boast of his riches; but let him who boasts boast of this, that he understands and knows Me, that I am the Lord who exercises lovingkindness, justice and righteousness on earth; for I delight in these things," declares the Lord* (Jeremiah 9:23-24).

Allegiance is based on an understanding of the King's kingdom and the rewards of the Promise-Keeper. This promise is real to real to my people and their boast is truly in Him. The glory of these realities at times appeared to be more real to the people in the war zone than those in nations where peace, civil order, and security were taken for granted. Daily life in wartime Baghdad was marked by explosions, missiles, hidden car bombs, and constant bloodshed. Fear and anxiety pervaded the atmosphere, food was scarce, public services closed down, and the infrastructure of the nation began to disintegrate. In this climate, the people fervently appropriated and embraced the assurances of the kingdom, particularly the Beatitudes. The Beatitudes were not just consoling verses from the blessed holy Nazarene; they were the attributes of an unbreakable covenant. The beatitudes were legally binding life insurance papers, penned by a holy, just, and righteous Judge—signed and sealed by the blood of the King.

> Oh, you never have to be afraid of joining yourself to this Nazarene, for he is always a King. When Jesus was

dying he was a King.... Thank God, it is finished, and I
know that because it is finished, everything is mine—
things in heaven, things on earth, things under the
earth. Jesus Christ is all power over all. He is all in all.
He is through all. Thank God, he is for all.[4]

The greater our revelation is of the majesty and kingship of
Jesus, the greater our sense of allegiance will be. It was Daniel's
awareness of the majesty, splendor, and sovereignty of the God of
Israel that enabled him to be allegiant and to withhold any trace of
allegiance, even in his daily diet, to the Babylonian king.

Saddam Hussein owned lions and tigers that he kept in cages
so that people whose political or moral persuasion were not in
accord with his could be thrown in there to be eaten by the animals. The animals themselves were treated terribly and their only
food was literally people. The animals had no other food until after
Saddam's death when the national zoo was restored and financed.
When I reflect on the horrors of the regime, I am reminded of
King Nebuchadnezzar, who defied the living God and barbarically
persecuted those he perceived as rebels with fire and wild beasts.
Along with countless others, this ancient Babylonian tyrant could
be compared to several evil dictators in modern history. On many
levels we see history repeating itself, yet the question remains—
how do we respond? Our engagement with political affairs,
judicial governance, and social justice is paramount. The church
must take ground, lead, influence, and reform, yet at the same time
we must be like Daniel. We must set our faces toward the heavenly
Jerusalem and steady our gaze on the King of the kingdom. We
must pray fervently for the sovereignty and wisdom of God to be
manifest in our midst.

As I mentioned, one of the keys to our living in the glory zone was constant worship in the face of suffering. We had no choice but to steady our gaze on Heaven like Daniel did, and we had to adopt Jehoshaphat's position, which was one of radical worship during times of desperation. For each of us, whenever we share bread and wine, declare His resurrected body, worship Him with flags and banners, and acknowledge His worth, we are reconfirming allegiance. This allegiance flows from a reverence rooted in deep love. The Greek word *thréskeia* used by James, the brother of Jesus, when referring to "true undefiled religion" literally means "reverence" and "fear of the Lord." The Spirit of the Reverent Fear of the Lord empowers allegiance by illuminating the worth of Jesus. Seeing His majestic worth enables us to stand boldly and unashamedly before Him, even to the point of death.

> *Women received back their dead by resurrection; and others were tortured, not accepting their release, so that they might obtain a better resurrection; and others experienced mockings and scourgings, yes, also chains and imprisonment. They were stoned, they were sawn in two, they were tempted, they were put to death with the sword* (Hebrews 11:35-37).

Every time we worship, whether dancing before Him, kneeling at His feet, or lying prostrate on the floor, we are choosing to stand. We are not standing through the strength and passion of stoic devotion; we are standing *in* the victory of the King. As I mentioned in another chapter, we are hiding in His name: *"Moses built an altar and named it The Lord is My Banner"* (Exod. 17:15). We are laying our lives on the altar of sacrifice and wrapping ourselves in the King's flag that showcases the words "it is finished."

Is it not beautiful to think that the transition from earth to Heaven can be one of worship? Is it not wonderful to think that there does not need to be a break in the middle between death and eternal life? Is it not overwhelming to think that we can pass from the environment of Heaven that we have cultivated on earth straight through a green light into the place that He has prepared for us?

The word *martyr* is used in the New Testament, and the original Greek word means "witness" and "bearing testimony." It relates to those who have loyally carried the testimony of Jesus and remained steadfast to His Word:

> *When the Lamb broke the fifth seal, I saw underneath the altar the souls of those who had been slain because of the word of God, and because of the testimony which they had maintained...and I saw the souls of those who had been beheaded because of their testimony of Jesus and because of the word of God* (Revelation 6:9; 20:4).

A martyr is someone who is persecuted or who suffers due to their religious or political beliefs. It is not a common word in Western culture outside of history books as it is not a common phenomenon in peaceful, democratic, protected societies where religious freedom and cultural tolerance are promoted. Nevertheless, we are all faced with choices of how to respond when we are victimized. As American speaker and author Iverna Tompkins states in one of her sermons entitled "What Now?":

> The early disciples were people of persecution, their faith did not keep them out of trouble, it kept them in

trouble all the time! Often what we call persecution is getting a dent in our Rolls Royce, but the fact is that we may yet go through some real persecution but "my strength," He says, "is made perfect in weakness."[5]

Generally, in the West we have no grid for the type of persecution suffered by the early church, as it is not part of our experiential landscape. Furthermore, we would all agree that death, torture, and suffering are not desirable topics to contemplate or discuss. Terrorism, however, has affected almost all of our Western nations, and we have all witnessed modern suicide bombers blindly attempt to define themselves as "God-fearing martyrs." We have all witnessed the level of distortion and perversion in the application of the word *martyr* to those who have bought into the hellish deception that blowing oneself up and simultaneously murdering thousands of innocent civilians is an act of faith and martyrdom.

True martyrdom is born from divine love. Terrorism is born from demonic hatred. Martyrdom relates to being transfixed upon the living God. Terrorism relates to the hate-filled denouncement of His name. Martyrs do not love their life unto death. Terrorists love death unto death. When we look at scripture and consider the martyrdom of Stephen, we see that his strength was where his gaze was set. His death was a radiant death. Stephen saw the King in all His glory seated at the right hand of the Father. Stephen was unwaveringly convinced of the identity and preeminence of Christ and could walk with courage, conviction, and intentionality into a violent death.

But being full of the Holy Spirit, he gazed intently into heaven and saw the glory of God, and Jesus standing at the right hand of God; and he said, "Behold, I see the heavens opened up and the Son of Man standing at the right hand of God" (Acts 7:55-56).

Stephen's face was glowing as he saw into Heaven. As he opened his mouth to speak, he was already experiencing the glory zone within the war zone. Our ability to withstand persecution, hatred, and "enragement of others" due to our faith in Jesus (whatever form this may take) relates to the strength of our gaze. Who are our eyes fixed on? Who are we? Are we aware of our true identity? Have we remembered our heavenly location as being seated above with Jesus?

> *Our citizenship is in heaven, from which also we eagerly wait for a Savior, the Lord Jesus Christ* (Philippians 3:20).

My prayer is that in every nation across the globe, rich or poor, peaceful or war-torn, God raises up a forceful army of overcomers who sound the trumpet call of victory: *"because of the blood of the Lamb and because of the word of their testimony."* I pray too that we continue learn the true meaning of allegiance from who those who *"did not love their life even when faced with death"* (Rev. 12:11).

As we read on in the book of Acts, we see how the persecution of Stephen led to widespread violence and suffering in the region and resulted in a scattering of the saints. Yet God was in control and these scattered seeds created a harvest across the Roman Empire leading to the establishment of the early church. The spiritual solidarity, collective testimony, harmony, and widespread intercession formed a mighty power surge, an invincible spiritual ground and air force, and the church became expansive, impactful, and fortified in and through times of severe persecution.

> *So then those who were scattered because of the persecution that occurred in connection with Stephen made their way to Phoenicia and Cyprus and Antioch, speaking the word to no one except to Jews alone. But there were some of them, men of Cyprus and Cyrene, who came to Antioch and began speaking to the Greeks also, preaching the Lord Jesus. And the hand of the Lord was with them, and a large number who believed turned to the Lord* (Acts 11:19-21).

My prayer for our remaining Iraqi community who are gradually acquiring visas to other nations (having crossed into safety from Iraq into Jordan) is that in dispersion and scattering, revival fires will be ignited. My prayer is that we experience powerful results of the same standard and caliber as the early church—a situation where *"those who had been scattered went about preaching the word"* (Acts 8:4).

I have seen an overwhelming sense of oneness in Christ arise from their suffering and I have seen walls of tradition collapse, and religious differences within the wider Christian Iraqi community completely dissolve. I have watched God activate a complete disintegration of denominational barriers and replace it with a reintegration of different groups into the totality of His love. As I pray and ponder the road ahead, I am certain that the testimony of their faith will impact those nations in which they now live. I pray that fires of deep love and allegiance will be ignited as testimonies are voiced—testimonies of God's goodness; accounts of signs, wonders, miracles, angels, visions, encounters; or, indeed, stories of loved ones who loved Jesus unto death.

This was the essence of the early church—glory and persecution. As we see clearly both in the vivid accounts of the crucifixion and resurrection of Jesus and in the death of Stephen, glory and persecution often go hand in hand and have done so throughout the ages. For the redeemed there is no mortality, only eternity with King Jesus. He is our pledge and His promise to us is based on the eternal blood covenant.

> *Now He who establishes us with you in Christ and anointed us is God, who also sealed us and gave us the Spirit in our hearts as a pledge* (2 Corinthians 1:21-22).

When we consider how Christ obligated Himself to be our kinsman redeemer and was allegiant to the point of death, we realize that the standard is set by Him. Loyalty is in His very nature: *"Loyalty and truth preserve the king, and he upholds his throne by righteousness"* (Prov. 20:28)

His name is *Faithful and True*, and we have been created as co-heirs of Him. He is a faithful priest and the mediator of an eternal covenant that signs and seals the redemption and eternal life of all who pledge allegiance to Him. The priesthood of Jesus offers a legal, assured, eternal future for all who believe in His name.

> *(...He with an oath through the One who said to Him, "The Lord has sworn and will not change His mind, 'You are a priest forever'"); so much the more*

also Jesus has become the guarantee of a better covenant (Hebrews 7:21-22).

It is this absolute assurance of divine love that offers confidence, comfort, and consolation to those who face persecution. Paul's exhortation to the early Christians who were being ravaged and terrorized by enemy forces was focused neither on a call to stoic resilience nor on an exhortation to self-defense. Solidarity and future legacy were crucial; loyalty and fidelity of the persecuted ones was necessary for the continuation of future generations, yet none of these factors formed the thrust of Paul's exhortation and appeal.

> *Who will separate us from the love of Christ? Will tribulation, or distress, or persecution, or famine, or nakedness, or peril, or sword? Just as it is written, "For Your sake we are being put to death all day long; we were considered as sheep to be slaughtered." But in all these things we overwhelmingly conquer through Him who loved us. For I am convinced that neither death, nor life, nor angels, nor principalities, nor things present, nor things to come, nor powers, nor height, nor depth, nor any other created thing, will be able to separate us from the love of God, which is in Christ Jesus our Lord* (Romans 8:35-39).

There were many values to which Paul could have passionately drawn the minds of the people, yet he had learned that the only revelation necessary was that of God's love. The foundational, life-giving truth is the unconditional love of Christ and the nearness of the Father who cannot be distanced by systemic evil or the bloodthirsty crimes of violent men. His love is with you in the war zone; He is with you in the line of enemy fire.

In Baghdad we saw that the Father's love was not distanced by onslaughts of demonic activity or by the terrorizing sounds of enemy fire. Even during the darkest hours of bloodshed when we wept with grief and sorrow, we knew the sound of His voice to be stronger than the haunting cries of slaughtered civilians.

I value what Patricia King refers to as "the throne zone" as, for me, this is another name for "the glory zone." Part of the reality of experiencing the throne zone is about interceding for the establishment of its foundations in our midst—justice and righteousness. It is about living with a royal perspective and kingdom mindset. This was easy for Christians to grasp in Baghdad because the whole notion of "throne" was central to living everyday life under a dictator. They understood and thanked God for the more powerful regime, the superior reign, the existence of a singular benevolent sovereign whose reign was one of righteousness, justice, joy, and peace.

We must always remember that the throne is a *throne of grace*, and we must intentionally transfix our gaze upon the Lamb seated upon this throne. Revelation increases as we give Him our gaze for therein is the fullness of glory.

There are times when each of us experiences a level of "Gethsemane" (the place of the "olive press"). During these moments of darkness, solitude, confusion, pain, and turmoil, it is the revelation of Jesus and His glory that remains our lifeline, our hope, and our reason to endure.

> *The Spirit Himself testifies with our spirit that we are children of God, and if children, heirs also, heirs of God and fellow heirs with Christ, if indeed we suffer with Him so that we may also be glorified with Him* (Romans 8:16-17).

During my years in the war zone, the times of painful crushing produced a measure of fresh, pure oil and a unique type of anointing. The perpetual crushing and pressing released a distinct, fragrant aroma to our worship and a capacity to embrace more of Him. I believe that as the world enters some of its darkest moments, the worshiping community will become increasingly aware of the glory within them, the glory around them, and the glory that is to come.

> *For momentary, light affliction is producing for us an eternal weight of glory far beyond all comparison* (2 Corinthians 4:17).

Out of the painful crushing and pressing of the Iraqi believers came a glorious revelation of oneness in Christ, an increased awareness of the great ministry of light, and a sense of collective resolve to be intentional in worship and ensure that the lamp was always full of oil and ever-burning: *"Command the people of Israel to bring you pure oil of pressed olives for the light, to keep the lamps burning continually"* (Lev. 24:2 NLT).

We must remember that, in essence, it was the agonizing torture and humiliation endured by Jesus that produced and released the oil of Shavuot, the anointing of the Holy Spirit that flowed forth to all nations. Sorrow and mourning transformed into "the oil of gladness," and divine joy was released to the world.

Reflections

Blessed are those who have been persecuted for the sake of righteousness, for theirs is the kingdom of heaven. Blessed are you when people insult you and persecute you, and falsely say all kinds of evil against you because of Me. Rejoice and be glad, for your reward in heaven is great; for in the same way they persecuted the prophets who were before you (Matthew 5:10-12).

Regardless of how we are treated—whether in the workplace, the neighborhood, or the war zone—we must live in the completed victory of Jesus. We must stand firmly in the place of "it is finished."

In the world you have tribulation, but take courage; I have overcome the world (John 16:33).

True overcomers are ones who despite living out the apparent tension between "things unfinished" and "things finished" are able to reach above the pain of this tension and hold on to divine truth. What is this truth? It is the truth that victory over every form of evil was completed in Christ.

Prayer

Jesus, You assured us that those who know You, who carry Your Word, and do the will of Your Father have acted wisely by building their house upon a solid rock. I thank You for Your supreme faithfulness and for the certitude of Your promises. Whatever storms occur, no matter how ferocious or violent, we can rest in the knowledge that our lives have unshakable foundations in You. You do not leave us in the shipwreck, and You do not abandon us in the storm. You are our permanence, our peace, and our eternity; so, Father, cause every reader's eyes to be opened once again to the solidity of the rock that is higher than them.

Notes

1. Dietrich Bonhoeffer, *Letters and Papers from Prison*, ed. Eberhard Bethge, trans. Reginald Fuller (Minneapolis, MN: Fortress, 2015), 6.

2. Eberhard Bethge, *Dietrich Bonhoeffer: A Biography*, trans. Victoria Barnett, (Minneapolis, MN: Fortress, 2000), 927-928.

3. Dietrich Bonhoeffer, *The Cost of Discipleship* (New York, NY: Touchstone, 1995), 88.

4. Wigglesworth, *The Anointing of His Spirit*, 65.

5. Iverna Tompkins, "What Now?" YouTube (Gabriel Heights Telecasting, January 11, 2017), https://www.youtube.com/watch?v=ZaIPfqv_Qls.

CHAPTER FIFTEEN

GLORY IN THE WORD

THE IRAQI CHRISTIAN REFUGEE SCHOOL THAT WE STARTED in Amman adheres to the main components of the Jordanian education system. The learning of scripture is fundamental to their national educational curriculum, and Islamic children are expected to be able to recite the Quran and demonstrate sound religious knowledge. Biblical study is likewise a central part of the curriculum within the Christian schools that provide education to around five percent of the population.

In order to promote scriptural learning, the Ministry of Education holds an annual national Jordanian inter-school scripture recital competition. There are two separate fields to the contest—one for recital of the Quran (which comprises the majority of schools) and the other for the recital of the Bible. Each year our schoolchildren rise to the challenge of learning the New Testament word for word in Arabic and English. In-house recital competitions for parts of the New Testament take place through the year in order to prepare those who will represent the school in the national competition. Times of collective recital together are filled with enthusiasm and laughter, and much of the scripture is learned through song and drama. For three consecutive years now, our school has won the national inter-school competition reaching first place out of around twenty other Christian schools, winning the national award for biblical recital.

In an earlier chapter I described the reality and prominence of divine reversal in our midst. This is a further example of reversal as God transformed traumatized children (at risk of comparative failure when ranked against non-refugee children) into publicly recognized national champions. Despite the horrors of the past, our students have learned to hold their heads up high, bear the excellence of the King, and hide His Word deep within their hearts. They are children of the glory because they are "children of the Word." These young "lamp-carriers" understand that the Bible is a shining lamp unto their path, and my prayer is that they become part of the great company of blazing torch-bearers of the future.

More powerful still is the fact that the solar-powered Bibles that I mentioned in an earlier chapter continue to equip our students with the perfect methodology to learn the scriptures. They do not need to read arduous amounts of writing; they simply listen, absorb, meditate, and learn. The very asset that ISIS destroyed (the Word of God, their greatest weapon) has not only been restored to the children but is now the door to national honor and recognition. My heart rejoices when I see how, on a spiritual level, the holy Word of God that the enemy stole has not simply been repossessed but exists as the very means of God's consolation and vengeance. Glory-filled missiles of divine declaration are being unrelentingly fired back at the enemy through the mouths of infants who have learned to forgive their enemies and take their stand against darkness.

The fact that solar-powered audio Bibles had been given to me in both English and Arabic enables students to use them as a means of improving their English, which is imperative for the majority who are applying for asylum in English-speaking nations. The desire to be national champions, therefore, also improved the corporate standard of English within the school and raised confidence as the entire teaching and learning refugee community learned to see themselves from Heaven's perspective. The glory always affirms to us our identity and always replaces despair with joy because the glory is His presence, and in His presence there is fullness of joy.

The centrality of the Word was always a very real part of the glory zone in the war zone. In Baghdad, teenagers and adults used to come to Thursday and Friday night gatherings all with their own scripture to share. They would all have learned it by heart, having meditated on it before bringing it to share. I did not preach in those gatherings; the people preached together and to each other from the Word that they had hidden in their heart. Most shared Bibles and others learned from the audio Bibles if they did not have a hard copy.

What was always interesting to me was the fact that the most common scriptures that people treasured, shared, and felt God constantly illuminating were not the scriptures on rescue, deliverance, victory, and peace in our time, which one may expect people to cling to in the middle of the war zone. The most common scriptures that people would share together, cherish, and discuss were all scriptures on divine intimacy. People understood and valued the call and the privilege of living in intimacy with the Father, the Son, and the Spirit. I noticed that some of the most joy-inspiring passages for these dishonored and marginalized people were the scriptures from John on abiding in the Vine and the great invitation to fast with Jesus.

> *I stand at the door and knock. If you hear my voice and open the door, I will come in, and we will share a meal together as friends* (Revelation 3:20 NLT).

In the Middle East, sharing meals together is an intrinsic expression of friendship. It is the norm to eat together, show hospitality, open one's home, and cook food to share with others. Often the larger the crowd, the more joyous the event. Those who come and share a meal are not guests; they are friends. Having sufficient furniture is not an issue and guests are not counted like they are in the West; everyone floods into the house and eats—why? Because they are friends, they know each other, they love to share, and they recognize each other's voices. This was also the case on a spiritual level. Due to the simplicity of their lives and the scarcity of Bibles, the sharing of the Word was a daily reality. If the Word is bread, then bringing the Word to the table and partaking of it is a living, sustaining reality that is as real as literally sharing bread.

There was so much about the verse from Revelation above that my people loved and that we all love. It is a personal invitation into the glory zone. It is a request to dine with the King, and His voice is always calling. We must simply open the door to His friendship.

> *I am the vine, you are the branches; he who abides in Me and I in him, he bears much fruit, for apart*

from Me you can do nothing. ...Just as the Father has loved Me, I have also loved you; abide in My love. ...This is My commandment, that you love one another, just as I have loved you. Greater love has no one than this, that one lay down his life for his friends. You are My friends if you do what I command you. No longer do I call you slaves, for the slave does not know what his master is doing; but I have called you friends, for all things that I have heard from My Father I have made known to you. ...This I command you, that you love one another (John 15:5,9,12-15,17).

If biblical passages such as this had been all my people had managed to embrace, I believe it would have been sufficient to sustain them and keep them in a place of assurance and delight. These scriptures contain some of the greatest keys to intimacy, identity, and friendship with God, and they paint the greatest pictures of love as a person, love as a resting place, and love as an act.

In Western society many of us have a whole array of Bibles with concordances and versions lined up on our shelves. We have multimedia and multiple ways of receiving the Word; we live in "option overload" and often benefit from a constant stream of luxuries drip-fed to us by an immense well of diverse biblical resources. Yet what I have noticed is that many people in the West have never assimilated the Word and imbibed it into their being. For many, it is not "fashionable" to memorize, recite, contemplate, and experience the joy of unraveling and embracing the great scrolls that contain the eternal hope of the ages. It is one thing to march around one's calm, tranquil garden with a Bible in one's hand knowing that the declaration of the Word brings breakthrough (I have done this many times), but it is an entirely different thing to have the words deeply memorized and embedded in your heart.

The Iraqi Christians had an authentic hunger and thirst for the scriptures, and they knew the reality of being nourished and fortified by the indwelling Word. For those many people who were obliged to share Bibles due to the shortage, the pleasure of spiritually feasting together was a priceless luxury. Luxury was not perceived as a material ideal or a distant utopia; luxury was sitting together in safety reading scriptures, praying, and sharing a good meal together. Small groups that gathered around the one Bible available became edified and fortified as the sadness and insecurity caused by not owning a Bible was reversed by the strength and spiritual oneness of sharing.

The Iraqi children whose families fled Baghdad and who are now at our Iraqi refugee school in Jordan sing the Lord's prayer three times together every day. The majority of Westerners who visit the school comment on the spirit of worship and reverence that exists among them. Similarly, prayer and biblical recital are central to classes. Each class has their own special scripture that is "theirs," and they learn, sing, and recite it together. Taking ownership of the Word is so important, it becomes one's greatest treasure, one's most costly possession. The Word is ever-empowering, and it is untouchable for it lives within your spirit, the eternal part, the glory zone within. Whatever nation we live in and no matter how many Bibles we own, only the true faith-filled assimilation of the living Word enables us to cultivate the atmosphere of Heaven within ourselves and to carry this atmosphere wherever we go.

The Word carries its own glory because God is congruent with His Word and because the Word gives light. The glory zone is full of radiant light; it is saturated in light and no darkness can enter. We know that Heaven is full of blazing light, angels, fire, dazzling jewels, and that there is no need for a sun or a moon: *"And the city has no need of the sun or of the moon to shine on it, for the glory of God has illumined it, and its lamp is the Lamb"* (Rev. 21:23).

The same enlightenment is the light that beams forth and radiates from the Word. The Word *is* illumination, it *is* light, and wherever there is glory there is radiant light: *"Your word is a lamp to my feet and a light to my path"* (Ps. 119:105). We must ask God for a fresh revelation of the immensity of His light. The ministry of the Word is the ministry of light. All of us—young and old, rich and poor, Eastern and Western—must let it be the daily delight that satisfies us. *"How sweet are Your words to my taste! Yes, sweeter than honey to my mouth!"* (Ps. 119:103).

One recent year after I had left Baghdad and was spending longer seasons in Israel, I was speaking at Narkis Street Baptist Church in Jerusalem. While I was there, I met a group of children and early teens from Bethel Church, Redding. There were around fourteen children all between the ages of six and fifteen and were very excited as they were planning to be baptized in the Jordan. As they knew me from my visits to their community, they asked me to baptize them. I have baptized countless people of all ages and nationalities in the Jordan. So many of them have had a passion for Jesus; however, I will never forget this particular experience for one reason—there was an incredible wealth of scriptures hidden and treasured within these children. They did not have notebooks and Bibles with them at the riverbank, and some were as young as six years old, yet the level of scriptural content, prophetic unction, and spiritual caliber as they prayed the Word and prophesied over each other was outstanding. I had never seen anything like it in my life. The Spirit of Revelation was flowing and many wept and trembled as they spoke. Never in all of my time baptizing in the Jordan did I feel the atmosphere of glory surround me so quickly and physically as it did with the release of the Word from these children's lips. As the psalmist observed: *"The unfolding of Your words gives light"* (Ps. 119:130). As we recentralize the scriptures and give them their rightful preeminence in our lives, we will be able to cultivate and sustain a prophetic, life-giving culture in which all partakers can flourish and thrive.

Reflections

There is no glory outside of the Godhead. The glory is the fullness of His presence, and the Father *is* the Word, the Son is the Word made flesh, and the Holy Spirit is the Spirit of Glory.

> *If you are reviled for the name of Christ, you are blessed, because the Spirit of glory and of God rests on you* (1 Peter 4:14).

The Word of God *is* God. This is the majestic mystery of His personhood. The glory emanating from the Godhead or from His written and spoken Word are all mysteriously linked and part of our wealthy inheritance. This unfathomable truth was a survival technique to us in the war zone, yet I know we barely scratched the surface and there is infinitely more to experience.

If the divine scriptures are not alive, exuberant, and life-filled to you, if when you read you do not experience the daily nourishment of this living bread or the illuminating power of the Spirit enlightening your heart and mind to divine truth, then ask the Father to breathe upon His Word as you read. As He responds to your prayer, His Word will be life to you, and you will esteem it more precious than gold and silver as it minsters hope and light to every part of your being.

Prayer

Father, I ask that You forgive us for each time we have failed to cherish and embrace Your Word as we should. Thank You that Your Word is living and, as Jesus experienced Himself when confronted by the enemy in the wilderness, it is sharper than a two-edged sword. I thank You that Your Word is a bright shining lamp illuminating and enlightening the path before us even in the most challenging of circumstances. Father, I pray that the explosive truth of that which is written will come alive in the heart of every reader.

CHAPTER SIXTEEN

WORSHIP: HE IS WORTHY OF IT ALL

As the bishop states in Willa Cather's novel DEATH Comes for the Archbishop, "Where there is great love there are always miracles." I have realized the absolute surety of this statement in my work and ministry. Many would relate the statement to brotherly, fraternal love. I believe that while this is true, it is a secondary reality.

I believe that the real trigger for miracles is the expression of our love for the Godhead, which we can only do by first receiving His love. Our first call is to minister to Him and to love Him simply for who He is. Miracles did not abound in the war zone primarily because we loved each other. Miracles abounded because we worshiped Him and lived unitedly in His affection. The more we love on Jesus, the more we love each other, and the more we become the united expression of His heart on this earth.

Worship time for my congregation was adoration time. We kept Him as the object of our adoration, affection, and love. We learned to come with our incense offering amidst the smoke of war and to come with our voice offerings amidst the sounds of gunfire. As we did this, a realm of His presence opened up and the supernatural became real in our midst. The truth is there is more power in the faith-filled song of a weak believer than there is in a billion missile explosions. I am convinced of the superiority of our glory-filled sound waves and vibrations caused in the spiritual realm when we open our mouths and worship. This was a reality that I learned from my singing mother as a child. Wherever she went she sang to Jesus, and doors opened.

I truly believe that where there is great love, there are great miracles. During a war, people draw close in their courageous fight for survival, and brotherly love is not a great challenge. However, to stay in love with an invisible God who may appear to have forsaken you is a different story, and herein lies the challenge. We can only rise to the challenge by engaging in what I call "Jehoshaphat" moments. There are moments when like King Jehoshaphat we must stop, reposition, and fix our gaze exclusively on Him. This is the military posture of an army of Jesus-lovers. When we rose to the challenge and reset our gaze, we saw Heaven move on our behalf and God's manifest presence in our midst.

Jehoshaphat stood and said, "Listen to me, O Judah and inhabitants of Jerusalem, put your trust in the Lord your God and you will be established. Put your trust in His prophets and succeed." When he had consulted with the people, he appointed those who sang to the Lord and those who praised Him in holy attire, as they went out before the army and said, "Give thanks to the Lord, for His lovingkindness is everlasting." When they began singing and praising, the Lord set ambushes against the sons of Ammon, Moab and Mount Seir, who had come against Judah (2 Chronicles 20:20-22).

We learned to "send Judah first"—to worship first. We could not settle for living life in reaction to war, which demanded hatred of evil and vengeance of the enemy. We chose to live life in response to love. Often depleted and exhausted, we had to choose where to invest our energy, and we chose worship. As we centered on Jesus, we became reenergized by the motion of His love being poured back into us. Our worship band at St. George's Church was exceedingly modest when compared to many of the big worship bands of our day. Yet whether accompanied by piano, synthesizer, guitar, lute, or bongo-drum, our four vocalists and our enormous congregation certainly knew the joy of vibrant, exuberant, faith-filled worship. There was a holy revolution and a brave defiance to the resonance that they released through worship. Together their voices unleashed a new sound in the land.

Worship was mainly in Aramaic and Arabic with a few English songs thrown in the mix—the most classic of these being, "I have the joy...down in my heart." There was always lots of dancing and jumping. Three of our biggest joy-filled jumpers were a group of deaf and mute teenagers. These boys had tragically suffered from congenital syndromes that were commonly a result of chemicals from depleted uranium from the 1990 war. Many such children had been visited by Mother Theresa in 1993 when she visited Iraq and instantly commissioned three of her sisters to set up a care home for them. I would often visit the home and witness groups of deformed children singing together to Jesus. Meanwhile, the three famous "jumpers" back at St. George's Church just gave their all into jumping as high as possible and loved to be in a place of joy-filled celebration.

Worship, whether individual or corporate, always changes the atmosphere. Often in Thursday prayer and healing meetings we would feel a dramatic shift as people lifted up the name of Jesus and sang in their heavenly language. My people may not have had all the methodologies, guides, and course books that the average Western church member could access; however, I can confidentially say that such was the level of their adoration and trust, they were prepared to die worshiping.

I will always remember when a dear lady in our congregation, Evelyna, was healed of cancer within the atmosphere of the glory. Evelyna had been suffering from thyroid cancer for three years and had an extremely large goiter and various visible swellings as a result. Sadly, as was often the case, Evelyna could not afford surgery. Though we tried to cover the cost of all medical treatments, we simply did not have enough to pay the enormous costs of surgery for Evelyna. However, we did have free and immediate access to the most phenomenal surgical physician known to the Middle East, and everyone there knew him. His name is Jesus of Nazareth, and on that memorable Sunday during deep corporate worship, He reached out and touched Evelyna and she was immediately healed. She had come into church in her usual sad, swollen, weak physical state and left with a totally normal neck and a face full of joy. Our own medical team always sent everyone for complete medical checks, and we ran very thorough checks on Evelyna, which con-firmed that every trace of cancer had completely vanished.

Evelyna was a passionate intercessor and an active member of the Mothers Union. The Mothers Union, whom I mentioned earlier, was equipped with a kitchen and a room containing mul-tiple sewing machines, and 2,700 out of the 6,500 members of my congregation were members. Even young, single girls were desper-ate to gain membership. The attraction was not simply related to identity, solidarity, and united cause; it was the level of God's pres-ence and the endless reports of divine supernatural occurrences that emerged from within the union. Baghdad was in fact home to the most powerful wing of the Mothers Union abroad. Even I became a member of the Mothers Union and accompanied women to dangerous areas where together we took care of the despised and rejected and gave them food, garments, audio Bibles, and pastoral care.

In times of crisis, women moving in the anointing of the Spirit are powerful. Consider the great acts of Deborah and Esther whose voices amidst crises broke through and released change. In Middle Eastern culture, men are served and women serve. Men are consid-ered power-holders, and woman are often considered to be useful but powerless. Yet in the glory zone everything changes. The Iraqi women prayed relentlessly with unwavering faith, and they served day and night meeting the practical needs of the people. They stood united as Mary and Martha combined, and their ministry caused great tidal waves often leading to a greater manifestation of the kingdom than was seen elsewhere. Their devotion to the King of Glory opened up the realm of miracles. Servanthood and sover-eignty cannot be separated. Servanthood releases the manifestation of kingship because "the greatest in the kingdom is the servant of all." We must honor the women in our midst, and God forgive us if ever we have underestimated the centrality of their role in releasing the presence of Jesus.

In 2010 before the ISIS invasion, we experienced various bombings from faction groups consisting of Sunni and Shia radicals—many of these Sunni radicals would later form ISIS. They came from Al Anbar, near the town of Tirkrit (the birthplace of Saddam Hussein), a region known as the Sunni triangle. As I mentioned earlier, half of my embassy congregation were military men and half were diplomats from the state department. One Saturday evening not long after we began the chapel service (held in a hut in the embassy grounds), the sirens began to blast. We were about halfway through the worship service when suddenly the piercing sound of the emergency sirens started to blare and a whole stream of mortars started landing in the embassy area. They were landing within twenty feet of the chapel and within minutes we became literally surrounded by explosions. Right there in the midst of praise and worship, every person apart from me immediately fell to the floor (I remained in my chair as it was difficult for me to move quickly). This was how we had been trained to respond in crisis— lie face down on the floor. Could this crisis position speak of one of the best spiritual postures for us to adopt in times of crisis? It was while in this position of surrender and "hiddenness" before the Ark that Samuel realized God was not absent but very present.

Our worship leader in the embassy congregation during that time was an African American of the 101st Airborne Division named Winston. Winston was a very joyful-spirited man of God from Alabama and an anointed pianist. As rockets and mortars continued to land, Winston lowered himself to the floor and hid his head behind the piano; however, he refused to stop the worship, and in fervent desire to maintain the atmosphere he stayed kneeling on the floor and reached up his arms to the piano. He started to play the song "No Never Alone," and as he began to sing it (loudly and boldly, not softly as one might expect) a whole multitude of voices arose from the floor. It was a great Jehoshaphat moment—when you do not know what to do, let Judah lead the way. As I sat on my chair learning this song for the first time, I surveyed the bodies prostrate on the floor and became increasingly aware of a weighty glory that had suddenly entered the room as all of the voices mingled. It was like a heavenly mist that rested upon the people as they lay low and sang. I was amazed by the fact that the people were responding in the only possible way to respond. Theory had become reality and we felt a wave of divine love enter the chapel causing fear to diminish. As you can imagine, we did not arrive at the preaching part of the service, yet we did experience one of the most powerful worship times of my whole ministry in Baghdad. Jesus was in our midst and Jesus is the best preacher. We could sense the presence of angels and we knew that we were not alone:

> No, never alone, no, never alone,
>
> He promised never to leave me,
>
> never to leave me alone.
>
> —LUDIE PICKETT, 1897

The mortars continued landing for thirty minutes and the emergency sirens continued for over an hour. Once the sirens stopped, everyone arose from the floor and prudently left the building.

Reflections

To this day, whenever I meet people who were there on that memorable Saturday evening in Baghdad, they recall the "Never Alone" moment as being the "moment of moments" when we experienced the protective presence of the Almighty in such a powerful way. As faith-filled worship arose from the floor, we experienced the fullness of being in the glory zone within the war zone.

Whatever you may be facing right now, whether you live in a war-torn nation or whether the terror surrounding you relates to disease, bankruptcy, depression, rejection, or intimidation, you too may feel paralyzed and want to lie and bury your head on the floor. I am not here to tell you that trials will instantly diminish and that your situation is on the verge of radical, sudden change; however, I am here to tell you that you are never alone. God has not abandoned you and He will give you a brave heart. In the most dreadful, tormenting, and soul-crushing of predicaments, His glory is there for you. His glory is always there in Gethsemane. You must keep singing the name of Jesus and you must not stop. If you are too weak to sing yourself (as at times I was) ask friends to sing His name over you.

Prayer

Father, I thank You that faith-filled praise and abandoned worship transform the atmosphere and release tsunami waves of Your presence. I thank You that as Paul and Silas experienced, our worship attracts angels, breaks chains, opens doors, and releases the activity of Heaven. Father, I ask that by Your Spirit You move each one of us into new realms of worship as we fix our eyes on Jesus. I pray that You would show yourself strong on behalf of all those reading and increase their awareness of the depths of Your affection toward them.

CHAPTER SEVENTEEN

THE GLORY OF THE SHEPHERD

A shepherd should pay close attention to
the faces of his flock and hold close to his
heart the condition of those he cares for.
—PROVERBS 27:23 Passion Translation

GOD HAS BEEN SPEAKING TO ME RECENTLY ABOUT "THE
glory of the shepherd." It is not a common theme or title, but a
word that I have been carrying in my heart for a while. We hear a
lot about the fivefold ministry, and in many circles it is somewhat
fashionable to overuse the titles of apostle, prophet, teacher, evangelist, and pastor. They are titles that describe highly important
God-ordained ministry functions, but at times I have seen them
thrown around as if they were a fashion label or a trademark.

Though I was raised largely Pentecostal, when I heard God calling me to be a voice within the Anglican church, the titles attributed to my role were "curate," "vicar," and then "canon," which is a term used for those who work in a cathedral. However, I never allowed either these titles or the biblical ministry titles attributed to my role by those in charismatic circles to be an issue to me. What matters is that which God has seeded and nurtured in our hearts and the way in which we cultivate an ability to hear Him and flow with Him into the fullness of our call.

Interestingly, I was born on June 29, on what is known by the traditional Gregorian church calendar as St. Peter and Paul's Day. Insofar as Paul was the main apostle to the Gentiles and Peter was the main apostle to the Jews, the apostolic nature of my work in Israel and Iraq to Jews and Gentiles bears an interesting link to the day on which I was born. I always knew that I was a "sent one," and throughout my ministry I became acutely aware of the people to whom I was sent. In my opinion, this is really all that matters—we ought not look to titles and labels to validate our call or to establish our sense of worth.

In Iraq and Jordan, all of my people call me *Abouna*, which means "Father," and in essence this is what I consider myself. I am the spiritual father of a large family—whether dead or alive, localized or dispersed, citizens or refugees, my people are my covenant family. For me this is the most comfortable of titles to carry as it defines the real me.

Now, though, I want to share a little of what God has spoken to me about the glory of the Shepherd. The title of "Shepherd" is not commonly used nor does it carry the panache, authority, and prestige that the fivefold ministry titles may appear to carry. Yet I can assure you that it is one of the most Jesus-filled roles that one can assume. It is a role charged with great duty and responsibility, one that the eye of God watches carefully. Throughout the history of Israel, we see constant divine warnings, reprimands, and exhortations voiced by the prophets toward the spiritual shepherds. Through Nahum, God reprimands them for laziness; through Zechariah and Zephaniah, God warns them against causing the people to wander without a vision and leaving them vulnerable to worshiping idols and following foreign gods that in turn will become godless shepherds: *"Woe to the worthless shepherd, who deserts the flock!"* (Zech. 11:17 NIV). Isaiah rebukes the shepherds for lacking understanding and showing no thirst for knowledge while referring to them as greedy and selfish. God was always concerned with the welfare of His flock, and His desire has always been that they be led into all truth.

It is significant that the greatest Israeli king (who was a type of the Messiah) was anointed for kingship while he was a shepherd. David had learned foundational truths relevant to the role of leader, protector, and carer before he ever started to lead people. As a shepherd, he had his first encounters with the glory of God, and as a shepherd he cultivated a tender heart to live and lead from a place of clarity and truth.

Let us now consider the shepherds in Bethlehem who were perceived as the most unlikely to see the glory of God yet were considered worthy to receive the great scroll of Heaven regarding the announcement of the King's birth. When one reflects on this, it is quite astonishing. Shepherds were the last group of people the priests and rabbis would have expected important news to be delivered to, let alone news announcing a royal birth. How could one entrust the details of the birth of the Messiah to a mere group of uneducated peasants?

> *There were some shepherds staying out in the fields and keeping watch over their flock by night. And an angel of the Lord suddenly stood before them, and the glory of the Lord shone around them; and they were terribly frightened. But the angel said to them, "Do not be afraid; for behold, I bring you good news of great joy which will be for all the people; for today in the city of David there has been born for you a Savior, who is Christ the Lord. This will be a sign for you: you will find a baby wrapped in cloths and lying in a manger." And suddenly there appeared with the angel a multitude of the heavenly host praising God and saying, "Glory to God in the highest, and on earth peace among men with whom He is pleased."*
>
> *When the angels had gone away from them into heaven, the shepherds began saying to one another, "Let us go straight to Bethlehem then, and see this thing that has happened which the Lord has made known to us." So they came in a hurry and found their way to Mary and Joseph, and the baby as He lay in the manger. When they had seen this, they made known the statement which had been told them about this Child. And all who heard it wondered at the things which were told them by the shepherds. But Mary treasured all these things, pondering them in her heart. The shepherds went*

back, glorifying and praising God for all that they
had heard and seen, just as had been told them
(Luke 2:8-20).

The timing of God was perfect; the newborn king would
be identified and located by shepherds. These shepherds would
become the first set of evangelists to the Temple. There faces would
have been known for their sheep were used for Temple sacrifices.
The shepherds and their flocks beheld the glory of angelic worship, the glory of the message, and the glory of the newborn king.
Upon the heads of these men was bestowed the highest of honors
and to them was imparted the most sacred of secrets. Within a war-
torn, occupied Israel, the glory and majesty of God broke in and
changed the course of history. On that sacred day as they beheld
the angelic voices in their fields and journeyed to the cave to find
the child, the shepherds became swept up out of the war zone into
the glory zone.

These shepherds would never have dreamed that they were
about to be accompanied by the hosts of Heaven. The idea would
have been unthinkable and absurd. Yet to them was given the
honor of seeing the newborn Lamb, who Himself was to enter
humanity and live life both as a Shepherd and as a Lamb.

Shepherding was a tough life. The sheep were the object of
the shepherds' affection and grew quickly to recognize the voice
of their leader. They were totally dependent on good shepherding and vigilant protection from the wild beasts and vultures that
awaited their prey. During the winter season, the shepherds kept
their flocks in the valleys, and in summer they moved them to
the mountain pastures. The shepherds used the stones to make

sheepfolds and at times depended on natural caves and enclosures. Their work was hard and often unseen.

The flocks were fed through winter on a mixture of chaff and barley, and small flocks of twelve or less were often entrusted to a younger shepherd; however, many flocks and herds consisted of thousands and demanded skill and attention. Shepherds were acquainted with solitude, standing alone in vast open spaces under the sky, leaning on their crooks. Many Jews saw this as a dubious trade and an ignoble calling, never to be taught to one's son.

Watching over immense flocks demanded a high level of care and attention. Many sheep tried to wander astray, and wild beasts such as hyenas, jackals, wolves, and bears were common. Shepherds were always armed with a solid iron-bound cudgel and a large knife as they were surrounded by potential danger. Meanwhile, the burning midday heat and biting night frost meant a rough living. Shepherds wore thick woolen cloaks to cover them during the bitterly cold nights, and many grouped together bringing their flocks to the same place in the evening so that each shepherd could watch in turn and allow the others to sleep in the tent. To make the watching easier, the shepherds built huge sheepfolds with drystone walls high enough to prevent escape.

Many of the pasture grounds had watchtowers in them similar to those built in vineyards. Robbers and bandits were also a constant threat. As the shepherds led the sheep to drink in the morning, they uttered piercing cries that the sheep would recognize and played a reed pipe or flute as they walked with the flocks. The shepherds also had to take good care of any sick and injured sheep, ewes that were soon to give birth, and newborn lambs.

I could continue with my description, but the picture is clear. Shepherds were not valued, and a significant amount of their work was unseen. They were looked down upon by many, yet theirs was a life marked by duty and affection. Sheep would even come to the call of their own names, and if one got lost the shepherd would be anxious and immediately set out to retrieve it. The lost sheep would be relentlessly searched for and carried back to the flock on the shepherd's shoulders.

I am sure that many involved in church leadership would agree that aspects of the above description could easily be applied to their own life and to their flock. The role of a shepherd is a high call; true shepherding demands time, energy, hard work, attentive observation, sacrifice, persistence, endurance, discernment, insight, vigilance, astuteness, and deep compassion. Yet I truly believe that the call of the shepherd is one of the highest calls and, indeed, a glorious call.

Jesus Himself was often addressed by those to whom He spoke as "Rabbi" and also "Great Teacher." Yet one of the most frequent titles that He attributes (explicitly and implicitly) to Himself other than as the "Son of Man" is "Shepherd." I do not believe this was simply because shepherds and their flocks were common to the Israeli landscape and that it was an ideal metaphor to use. I believe that the very heart of Jesus was and is the heart of a shepherd.

> *I am the good shepherd; the good shepherd lays down His life for the sheep. ...I know My own and My own know Me, even as the Father knows Me and I know the Father; and I lay down My life for the sheep. I have other sheep, which are not of this*

fold; I must bring them also, and they will hear My voice; and they will become one flock with one shepherd (John 10:11; 14-16).

Unlike those spiritual leaders in Israel's past who allowed the glory to depart and the people to wander aimlessly, the leadership of Jesus is perfect. Peter knew this well and describes his master as the "chief shepherd." His message to those pastors (spiritual shepherds) of the early church is to stay faithful and vigilant to the end for the shepherd's rewards will be great.

And when the Chief Shepherd appears, you will receive the unfading crown of glory (1 Peter 5:4).

It is beautiful to me when I consider the ascension ministry of Jesus to see that though He is Sovereign King in majestic splendor seated at the right hand of the Father, His identity as both Lamb and Shepherd continues on as a heavenly reality. When Jesus returns, He will return as King and He will return as Chief Shepherd.

For the Lamb in the center of the throne will be their shepherd, and will guide them to springs of the water of life; and God will wipe every tear from their eyes (Revelation 7:17).

God spoke to me constantly through the different landscapes and cityscapes of Baghdad. Unlike towns in the West, there were sheep walking around the roads, often aimlessly in the middle of traffic, which was forced to drive around them. It was normal to see sheep walking in public pathways at the side of roads. There were shepherds around, but I never knew what the aim of these men was. They were not taking the sheep to pasture as there were no green fields around. In fact, there was no green whatsoever in sight. The street shepherds were always very scruffy and dirty and usually had a stick.

The sheep that roamed the towns in flocks were rarely alone, but they always looked sad. They fed on rotting garbage and drank from drainage gutters and whatever puddle they could find around the water pipes. It was heartbreaking for me coming from a homeland that has so much rich, verdant, agricultural activity, so much rural beauty—abounding in magnificent green scenic landscapes, rolling green hills, and pasturelands—to see gray, skinny, Iraqi sheep looking so neglected and unkempt within a habitat that was clearly not their own. These sheep were forced to live like pigs surrounded by trash and rubble, unable to embrace the plenitude and tranquility of the natural environment for which they had been created. Occasionally, I would stop and stroke them or cuddle them close to me and I would think of the tenderness of Jesus.

Seeing the people, He felt compassion for them, because they were distressed and dispirited like sheep without a shepherd (Matthew 9:36).

At night the sheep were left in a concrete compound with water pots. Newborn lambs would appear now and again, and they would follow the sheep, again looking gray, sad, and skinny. On a few occasions, in the very downtrodden suburb of Baghdad, I saw tiny lambs and I would pick them up and hold them close.

The daily experience of my surroundings caused me to contemplate the precious people whom God had entrusted to me. I found myself constantly praying that I would be a faithful shepherd and see to it that my flock was tenderly cared for, well-nourished physically and spiritually, and able to find a place of rest in God. My heart would sometimes break as I surveyed the roaming sheep and I pleaded with God that He would enable me to guide His people into truth and allow His name to be glorified within the danger zones of a nation at war.

Not long after I took over St. George's Church and initiated the renovation process, we transformed a dirt track outside our offices by planting grass seed and, later, building a seven-foot-high fountain there as a memorial to the death of Danish soldiers. It took just over a month for the grass to grow and the fountain that stood on the vibrant green lawn became a central place for outdoor worship gatherings. There was no other green grass to be seen in Baghdad, only here on our land. Every Friday the youth would have supper and worship around the fountain, which itself became a prophetic symbol of the presence of water within a dry land. When we gather around Jesus, we are gathering around the great well of living water, the great source of all life, the unending flow of His reviving presence.

> How precious is your lovingkindness, O God! And the children of men take refuge in the shadow of Your wings. They drink their fill of the abundance of Your house; and You give them to drink of the river of Your delights. For with You is the fountain of life; in Your light we see light (Psalm 36:7-9).

Several years later, one of the members of our congregation purchased two sheep for the community; the street shepherds charged fifty dollars each, and the two sheep came to live and graze on our church lawn. We called them Jacob and Isaac, named after the angora goats that I had in England. (I adored those goats, which had big shofars sticking out of their heads!) The gardener and caretaker ensured that our new fleecy additions to the church family were washed and nourished. Within a few weeks, they had transformed into clean, healthy, fat sheep. I would feed them special grains and nuts, and often when I was working at my computer on the lawn they would come and rub their heads against me. I felt as if they knew me and trusted me. Once I placed some chocolate in my hand. They came and sniffed it; however, they were not impressed.

These two sheep, Jacob and Isaac, turned into happy sheep and reminded me of the sheep in children's cartoons; they seemed peaceful and content in new surroundings that enabled them to graze in a place of love. This whole story speaks of the glory of the shepherd and the honor bestowed on those who are able to truly represent the sacrificial heart of the Chief Shepherd and carry His Spirit with tenderness and endurance. Even when I reflect on my permanent home address in England, which is "Shepherds Way," I sense Holy Spirit illuminating the call to prioritize, stay humble, and live my life the Shepherd's way. As I am reminded of the glory of this high call, I pray that in every nation God raises up faithful and attentive "street shepherds"—ones who will carry the glory outside of the church into the darkest areas of society. Of course, I include here the "shepherdesses" as much as the shepherds—those who, like Rachel, will gather, guide and nurture their Father's flock and thereby become a living expression of His heart. (*"Rachel came with her father's sheep, for she was a shepherdess,"* see Gen. 29:9). I pray that these brave shepherds learn to walk in the fullness of the anointing and unfailingly express the heart of God to those wandering aimlessly outside the protected zone.

During the ISIS invasions when people were fleeing for their lives, I promised my people I would never leave them. Some fled to Nineveh and further north to Erbil; however, most stayed together in Baghdad despite the dangers. When the massacre of Christians reached its peak, I was ordered by the Archbishop of Canterbury to leave before it became too dangerous to exit the country. During this time of my departure, most of my remaining congregation fled to Jordan, where I was reunited with them a few weeks later. Though their status has now changed from citizens to refugees, we had not left each other. They were and still are my flock, and I am still their spiritual shepherd. They know my voice and love to call me for chats. Those who emigrated to other continents and integrated into new church communities still call me for advice and time weddings and baby dedications around my international travel schedule.

A powerful example of my sheep knowing the sound of my voice took place not long after the war when I was passing through Dulles airport in Virginia in the US. I was sitting in the airport and near me was an African American lady who looked to be in about her mid-late 50s. As she caught my eye, I heard an inner, audible voice telling me to say to this lady: "You must name the baby Rivkah." I ignored the voice as it was too strange to be real and not many people would be calling their baby the Hebrew form of the name "Rebecca." However, the inner voice returned: "You must tell that lady to call the baby Rivkah." I heard the voice so clearly, but again I discarded it; the dear lady was clearly well beyond childbearing years and it seemed such a presumptuous and bizarre thing to say to a person whom one has never met before, let alone in the middle of an airport. However, the voice returned and, like Samuel, I heard the instruction for third time. By then I knew with certitude in my spirit that I needed to act.

I approached the lady and I said these words: "Good morning, Madam, call the baby Rivkah." The lady looked very shocked and asked me who I was. "I am just a pastor passing through," I replied.

"But how in this world did you know?" she asked.

"How do I know what?" I responded.

"My daughter is back home about to give birth and she has asked me to name the baby. I did not know what to choose and had been praying that God would confirm!"

The lady was overwhelmed and emotional, so I smiled and calmly repeated myself. "Call the baby Rivkah."

The lady then asked me to speak on the phone to her daughter who was at the hospital and literally in labor, soon to give birth. As soon as I said "hello," the daughter responded in amazement: "That's Abouna Andrew! It is you, isn't it, Abouna? I recognize your voice!" This was strange to me as she was not Iraqi, yet she was using my Iraqi title and referring to me as Father. I had no idea who she was and proceeded to ask her how she knew me. "I was in the American army in Baghdad," she replied. "You were my pastor for the eighteen months that I was part of your congregation at the embassy chapel."

Suddenly as she spoke on the phone, I remembered her name, recognized who she was, and began to relive those moments of worshiping together with the American military. She was overwhelmed that God had arranged for her pastor to name her baby and to pray with her as it was about to born. She and her mother had no idea of the gender, but a baby girl was born, and they called the baby Rivkah. What I cherish about this whole event is not so much the word of knowledge—though this itself was a treasure—nor was it the perfect timing and orchestration of God—though this indeed was wonderful and reflective of His goodness and loving-kindness. What speaks to me the most about this event was that God enabled a sheep to be mysteriously reunited to her shepherd. Furthermore, nothing had changed; the mutual love, honor, joy, and trust were still there, and the sheep recognized the voice of the shepherd.

We must never fail to see the shepherd's heart in every part of the Godhead. When blessing his sons, Jacob calls upon: *"the God before whom my fathers, Abraham and Isaac walked, the God who has been my shepherd all my life to this day"* (Genesis 48:15). David too recognized that God was in essence a shepherd; it was likely that David the shepherd-king wrote the twenty-third psalm in his later years. He really knew and understood the high, noble call of the shepherd as the attentive leader who protects, leads, refreshes, anoints with oil to keep away the flies, restores, provides, and loves.

> *The Lord is my shepherd, I shall not want. He makes me lie down in green pastures; He leads me beside quiet waters. He restores my soul; He guides me in the paths of righteousness for His name's sake. Even though I walk through the valley of the shadow of death, I fear no evil, for You are with me; Your rod and Your staff, they comfort me. You prepare a table before me in the presence of my enemies; You have anointed my head with oil; my cup overflows. Surely goodness and lovingkindness will follow me all the days of my life, and I will dwell in the house of the Lord forever* (Psalm 23).

The Son who is the Good Shepherd of the sheep also presents Himself as the gate and great entry point into the place of refreshment, rest, and rich satisfaction.

> *I am the door; if anyone enters through Me, he will be saved, and will go in and out and find pasture* (John 10:9).

When the Son ascended, returned to the Father, and spoke of the Holy Spirit, it was the shepherding heart of the Spirit that He highlighted—the faithful and steadfast person of the Father as represented through the person of His Spirit. There would be no need to fear flawed leadership, danger, ambiguity, or abandonment. There would be rich clarity and covenantal assurance even within the oppressive political climate of the hour. The Spirit would in this sense replace the Son and fulfil the role as the perfect, guiding Shepherd.

> *When He, the Spirit of truth, comes, He will guide you into all the truth; for He will not speak on His own initiative, but whatever He hears, He will speak; and He will disclose to you what is to come* (John 16:13).

When Jesus asked Peter about his love for Him, the standard of love that He expected from Peter was that of the shepherd. The true demonstration of Peter's love would be in his capacity to carry the shepherd heart.

Reflections

So when they had finished breakfast, Jesus said to Simon Peter, "Simon, son of John, do you love Me more than these?" He said to Him, "Yes, Lord; You know that I love You." He said to him, "Tend My lambs." He said to him again a second time, "Simon, son of John, do you love Me?" He said to Him, "Yes, Lord; You know that I love You." He said to him, "Shepherd My sheep." He said to him the third time, "Simon, son of John, do you love Me?" Peter was grieved because He said to him the third time, "Do you love Me?" And he said to Him, "Lord, You know all things; You know that I love You." Jesus said to him, "Tend My sheep" (John 21:15-17).

The greatest evidence of love, allegiance, and devotion to the Messiah relates to the cultivation and expression of this shepherd heart. It is not about glamour, stage, and fame; it demands the laying down of one's life. This is the very essence of the glory of the shepherd.

Prayer

Father, I bless every shepherd and I ask that You anoint them with fresh oil. I ask that they may know a heightened awareness of the high and noble call upon their life. I ask that every shepherd—whether in a megachurch, cyber church or home church—be filled with new levels of divine insight, wisdom, and energy.

For each person needing guidance, counsel, attention, and care, I ask, Father, Son, and Spirit, that You reveal to them Your Shepherd heart and that they experience the tender depths of Your love. I ask that those in a place of wandering and in search of a pasture and flock will be led by You to the place of refreshing and edification that You have prepared for them.

THE RIVER IN THE WAR ZONE

In the book of Samuel, we read of Israel's defeat by the Philistines. There was an initial loss of four thousand followed by a very heavy slaughter of thirty thousand men and widespread bloodshed in the land. The Philistines had been fearful that Israel had taken the Ark into the camp and were terrified by the sound of Israel's army. The Philistines rose up, defeating Israel, and took the Ark. (Two aspects the enemy hates the most—our carrying His presence and our battle-cry of praise.) After the news of Israel's hopeless defeat and the theft of the Ark, Phinehas, the daughter-in-law of Eli, gave birth to a son.

> *And when she heard the news that the ark of God was taken and that her father-in-law and her husband had died, she kneeled down and gave birth, for her pains came upon her. And about the*

time of her death the women who stood by her said to her, "Do not be afraid, for you have given birth to a son." But she did not answer or pay attention. And she called the boy Ichabod, saying, "The glory has departed from Israel," because the ark of God was taken and because of her father-in-law and her husband. She said, "The glory has departed from Israel, for the ark of God was taken" (1 Samuel 4:19-22).

As we read on, we see that the period following the theft of the Ark was marked by divine vengeance and severe wrath as God released "a heavy hand" of judgment upon Israel's enemies. When I read this account, I think of how the Ark represents those who carry the glory into war zones and how we are all carriers of the Ark, carriers of His presence. I reflect upon how the God of perfect justice will avenge the blood of the martyrs and judge evil in all its forms.

On many levels, the scene is a picture of how we felt in Baghdad during the time of terrorist invasion and ensuing bloodshed. Bibles were burned, children were beheaded, people were burned alive in cages; family properties, businesses, vehicles, fields, and livestock were ravaged and destroyed. There was a unified cry of "Ichabod"—where is the glory? "The glory has departed." I would be lying if I said that amidst the blood and turmoil this was not the cry of my own heart. I imagine Mary and the disciples felt the same as they watched Jesus hang on the cross, so brutally beaten and disfigured as the crown of thorns displayed that profound tension between *Kabod* and *Icahabod*—the "glorious" and the "un-glorious." Yet the eternal truth is that there is a third day. There is a day of restoration and resurrection, and this is the reality that must rule over the tension. Jesus Himself is the embodiment of that third day, for in all of the pain, anguish, and horror, He is the resurrection and the life. The truth is that for as long as we are with Him whether here or in Heaven, we need never cry "Ichabod." Why? Because He *is* the glory.

We can always live in the reality of the Risen King despite the dramatic tension between day one and day three, between pain and joy. For me personally, the river that flowed through Baghdad was a symbol of this tension.

> *The name of the third river is Tigris; it flows east of Assyria. And the fourth river is the Euphrates* (Genesis 2:14).

The Tigris is the second longest river in Iraq at a length of 1,150 miles, originating from the mountains in Eastern Turkey. The river flows through Syria and down to Iraq where it joins with the Euphrates to form the Shatt Al-Arab River. Ancient civilization thrived on the banks of the Tigris, and Baghdad stands on its banks. It is commonly used as a mode of transport, mainly for trade. It has close to fifty-five fish species. The fish population was much larger, but it declined drastically due to water pollution.

Our word *Tigris* (*Hiddekel* in Hebrew) comes from an Old Persian word that can be translated as "fast flowing" or "arrow-like" used by the ancient Sumerians who called the river *Idigna*. In the Akkadian language that was spoken in Babylonia and Assyria, its name was *Idiqlat*. In scripture it is referred to by Daniel as "the great river."

*On the twenty-fourth day of the first month, while I
was by the bank of the great river, that is, the Tigris,
I lifted my eyes and looked, and behold, there was a
certain man dressed in linen, whose waist was girded
with a belt of pure gold of Uphaz. His body also was
like beryl, his face had the appearance of lightning,
his eyes were like flaming torches, his arms and feet
like the gleam of polished bronze, and the sound of
his words like the sound of a tumult* (Daniel 10:4-6).

It is significant that the same river that flowed out of Eden,
the place of God's delight, was the river where Daniel experienced
such a level of divine revelatory flow. It is the place where centuries
before the Messiah's arrival, he saw visions of His glory just as his
contemporary Ezekiel did at the river Chebar. The connection is
profound, for at the very riverbanks of the river which had flowed
in purity from Eden, Daniel encountered He who would restore
the glorious perfection that was lost in the garden.

This was the very river that ran throughout Baghdad. As I
mentioned in Chapter Five, it was at the banks of the Tigris that
I had a deep experience with God's glory. However, these riverbanks were not simply a place of revelation but a place of great joy
and oneness. I always felt a deep connection with the river as it was
the place where I spent time with God early each morning. It was
for me a place of divine communion and friendship, a place where
I could walk alone with Jesus. Its banks were also the place of our
worship gatherings, church picnics, and parties. As a treat, I would
take the youth for dinners at the river where they ate the delicious
Iraqi huge fish (masgouf) that were cooked outside on an open
fire. The worship at the river was refreshing; there was a sense of

freedom and flow often greater than that experienced in corporate worship in the church building.

Yet this river of great moments, divine encounters, and ancient memories was also a place of agony. As ISIS moved in during the latter years, the Tigris—originally one of the four rivers of life flowing from Eden, a river of beauty in its purest form—became a river of death. Its waters became stained by human blood; it was the dumping place for rotting corpses, victims of brutality and persecution. The landscape of my morning prayer walks suddenly changed as one could see dead bodies, facedown, bobbing up and down in the water. The river darkened as body parts, broken debris, and military garbage littered the waters—the final sign of human degradation as dignity was stripped and citizens' rights to family burials were violated. The stench of evil and the presence of death toxified the waters as the river itself became the embodiment of the great tension of *Kabod* and *Ichabod*.

On a geo-ecological level, there have been restorative projects to clean and decontaminate the Tigris, and I pray that this restoration process is paralleled by a spiritual purging of the land. That is to say, we must pass beyond the natural river and reach into the superior reality of the King's river. The King's river is the rich, overflowing river of life that flows from His throne. It is the eternal life-sustaining river, and wherever this river flows everything lives.

> *It will come about that every living creature which swarms in every place where the river goes, will live. And there will be very many fish, for these waters go there and the others become fresh; so everything will live where the river goes* (Ezekiel 47:9).

The King's river is the place of lavish eternal blessing and rich flow of revelation. It restores dignity and self-worth, and on its banks are the trees that bring healing for the nations. As vitally important as they are, I do not believe for one moment that ecological restoration projects, humanitarian initiatives, elimination of post-dictatorial anarchy, and reestablishment of civil liberty will bring peace and healing to Iraq. Only the river of peace brings healing to the nations, only the presence of the King. It is in His nature to irrigate the dry places and to release cleansing, refreshing waters unto His people.

> *I provide water in the wilderness and streams in the wasteland, to give drink to my people, my chosen* (Isaiah 43:20 NIV).

The river of glory is a kingdom reality—the river flows from the throne, the place of sovereign rule. The currents of the river are quickened through worship, for worship establishes His throne and magnifies His majesty. The river flows inside of us.

> *Now on the last day, the great day of the feast, Jesus stood and cried out, saying, "If anyone is thirsty, let him come to Me and drink. He who believes in Me, as the Scripture said, 'From his innermost being will flow rivers of living water.'" But this He spoke of the Spirit* (John 7:37-39).

We must reembrace the reality of what we carry and unlock the currents within. We must tap into the power surge, eternal flow, dynamism, refreshment, purity, clarity, and momentum of

His presence. We must hold fast to this truth—there is a river in the war zone.

> *There is a river whose streams make glad the city of God, the holy dwelling places of the Most High* (Psalm 46:4).

This is an eternal river that we carry in us and that we are carried by. No matter what negativity you may experience in the natural, always remember there is a river in the war zone. This river is a place of energy, life, purification, refreshment, healing, tranquility, rest, and immersion. Whatever crisis comes your way, stay in the river. It is a river of divine glory whose currents are strengthened through intimacy with Jesus.

> What is the glory? All the glory that ever comes is from Jesus. You have the glory in the measure that you have the Son of glory in you. If you are filled with Jesus, you are filled with the glory.[1]

Note

1. Wigglesworth, *The Anointing of His Spirit*, 107.

About Andrew White

Canon Andrew White has served as a peacemaker and mediator engaging with key religious and political leaders in several nations, across differing faiths and denominations. He has a powerful apostolic ministry into the Middle East, particularly Israel and Iraq where he served for two decades and led a vibrant congregation of 6,500 people. Canon White's experience of life in sieges and war zones has been marked by signs and wonders and his deep desire is for all believers to know the glorious reality of being "one" in Jesus, our Messiah.

Printed by Printforce, United Kingdom